Gospel Light's

KIDS TIME

The Big Book of
Bible Skills

Gospel Light

HOW TO MAKE CLEAN COPIES FROM THIS BOOK

You may make copies of portions of this book with a clean conscience if

- you (or someone in your organization) are the original purchaser;
- you are using the copies you make for a noncommercial purpose (such as teaching or promoting your ministry) within your church or organization;
- you follow the instructions provided in this book.

However, it is ILLEGAL for you to make copies if

- you are using the material to promote, advertise or sell a product or service other than for ministry fund-raising;
- you are using the material in or on a product for sale; or
- you or your organization are **not** the original purchaser of this book.

By following these guidelines you help us keep our products affordable.

Thank you,
Gospel Light

EDITORIAL STAFF
Publisher, William T. Greig • **Senior Consulting Publisher,** Dr. Elmer L. Towns • **Publisher, Research, Planning and Development,** Billie Baptiste • **Managing Editor,** Lynnette Pennings, M.A. • **Senior Consulting Editors,** Dr. Gary S. Greig, Wesley Haystead, M.S.Ed.• **Senior Editor, Theological and Biblical Issues,** Bayard Taylor, M.Div. • **Editor,** Sheryl Haystead • **Contributing Writers,** Amanda Abbas, Mary Gross • **Contributing Editors,** Cathy Glass, Lisa Herman, Willamae Myers, Karen Stimer • **Designer,** Carolyn Thomas

CONTENTS

The Value of Good Bible Skills 4

How and When to Use This Book 5
The inside scoop on making the best use of the activities in this book.

The Bible—A Library of Smaller Books 6
An attractive page to help kids see at a glance the books of the Bible and the main divisions.

Bible Book Cards 7
Illustrated game cards for use in playing a variety of Bible games.

Bible Skills Activities 25
Games and more to help kids find their way around the Bible.
Identify and Spell Books
Put Books in Order
Identify Bible Divisions
Identify Key Phrases
Locate References

Bible Memory Activities 63
A variety of learning activities to encourage Bible memory.
Use these activities with any Bible memory verse.

Bible Skills Worksheets 93
Pages of fun to increase kids' knowledge of how the Bible is put together. (Answer Key on back of each page.)
Bible Characters
Bible Dictionary
Bible Word Definitions
Bible Books
Bible Divisions
Bible References
Map

Awards 167
Awards to motivate kids in learning Bible skills.

The Value of Good Bible Skills

Imagine sitting down at a computer, staring at a blank screen and knowing that all the information you need is right at your fingertips, YET YOU CAN'T ACCESS IT.

NOW IMAGINE the frustration level of children who are told that what they need is in the Bible, yet they don't know the first thing about finding their way around it.

It's common to drill young children to memorize their name, address and phone number; yet too often we neglect our responsibility to teach them how to get where they need to go in God's Word.

God's long-range goal for every child is that he or she may "reach unity in the faith and in the knowledge of the Son of God and become mature, attaining to the whole measure of the fullness of Christ" (Ephesians 4:13). Teaching students how to use the Bible equips them to grow and mature.

The beginning of this great process occurs as loving Christian adults work patiently, introducing God's Word through a variety of learning experiences that connect with each student's level of development and understanding. The activities in this book approach Bible skills in ways proven to engage kids—for example, games provide a way to make repetition fun and hook kids' interest to talk about scriptural meaning. The ultimate goal of all these activities is, of course, to focus not just on repetition or skill, but also on understanding that in turn results in desire for an ever-deepening relationship with God. Good Bible skills provide a foundation that—if begun well—will serve a person throughout an entire lifetime.

A FINAL WORD

Few things more effectively communicate the significance of God's Word to your students than the attitudes and actions of the adults around them. When students sense your enthusiasm for God's Word, they will come to value and respect God's Word. In addition to helping students learn skills in using the Bible for themselves, make sure you communicate ways in which God's Word helps you in everyday life.

How and When to Use This Book

IF YOU TEACH ALONE, start with these simple suggestions for encouraging the kids in your class to increase their Bible skills:

1. Provide Bible Skills Worksheets (pp. 93-166) for early arrivals to your classroom. Worksheets can also be completed by students who finish other activities early.

2. Lead students in a different Bible Skills Activity (pp. 25-62) during one session each month.

3. Prepare a Bible Memory Activity to help students memorize the memory verse suggested in your curriculum.

4. Prepare a set of Bible Book Cards (p. 7-23) along with the instructions for several games (pp. 27,33,45). Use them in class when time allows. Give cards and instructions to students to take home and play with family members.

IF YOU TEACH WITH ONE OR MORE other teachers, plan together how to use Bible skills activities:

1. Identify specific Bible skills your students need to develop, and plan times to lead students in appropriate activities. For example, if your students need help in locating Bible references, lead students to play "Name That Disciple" (p. 61) in class and provide each one with "Grapevine Lines" (p. 153) to complete at home.

2. Activities and worksheets can be substituted for or offered in addition to the activities suggested in your curriculum. Assign one teacher a Bible Skills Activity (p. 25-62) or Bible Skills Worksheet (p. 93-166) to prepare and provide for students during each session.

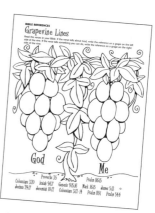

3. Plan an afternoon or evening pizza party with your students. Provide several active Bible Skills Activities such as "Ball Toss" (p. 28) or "Book Traders" (p. 38).

IF YOU ARE THE DIRECTOR or coordinator of several departments, here are still more ways to develop students' Bible skills:

1. Provide activities and worksheets for students during transition times between childrens' programs.

2. Provide Bible Skills Worksheets in packets or clipboards used by children during adult worship services.

3. Include the directions for several activities or games in the children's section of your church newsletter or in a children's ministry newsletter.

4. At a family camp or event, lead families to complete one or more Bible Skills Activities such as "Promise Search" (p. 55) or "People Scrabble" (p. 62).

5. During Sunday evening or weekday children's programs, establish a Bible Skills Learning Center at which students participate in one of the activities suggested in the book. Catch students' interest with an intriguing title such as "Take the Challenge." Offer awards to students who complete several Bible skills challenges such as completing a specified number of worksheets and participating in a certain number of Bible Skills and/or Bible Memory Activities.

THE BIBLE—A LIBRARY OF SMALLER BOOKS

NEW TESTAMENT

HISTORY

Acts

LETTERS BY PAUL To Others

First Timothy
Second Timothy
Titus
Philemon

PROPHECY
Revelation

GOSPELS

Matthew
Mark
Luke
John

LETTERS BY PAUL To Churches
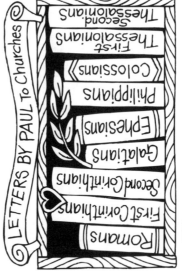
Romans
First Corinthians
Second Corinthians
Galatians
Ephesians
Philippians
Colossians
First Thessalonians
Second Thessalonians

GENERAL LETTERS
Hebrews
James
First Peter
Second Peter
First John
Second John
Third John
Jude

OLD TESTAMENT

HISTORY

Joshua
Judges
Ruth
First Samuel
Second Samuel
First Kings
Second Kings
First Chronicles
Second Chronicles
Ezra
Nehemiah
Esther

MAJOR PROPHETS

Isaiah
Jeremiah
Lamentations
Ezekiel
Daniel

THE LAW
Genesis
Exodus
Leviticus
Numbers
Deuteronomy

POETRY
Job
Psalms
Proverbs
Ecclesiastes
Song of Songs

MINOR PROPHETS
Hosea
Joel
Amos
Obadiah
Jonah
Micah
Nahum
Habakkuk
Zephaniah
Haggai
Zechariah
Malachi

How to Prepare Bible Book Cards

1. Photocopy pages 7-23 onto card stock or construction paper.

2. Laminate or cover pages with clear Con-Tact paper.

3. Cut cards apart using paper cutter or scissors.

4. Store cards in large manila envelope or resealable plastic bag.

Tips

1. Prepare several sets of cards for use in your classroom.

2. You may want to prepare a set of cards for each student to take home and use in reviewing Bible books.

3. Photocopy game directions and store them along with the appropriate Bible Book Card sets in envelopes or bags.

4. Invite volunteers to color cards with fine-tip markers before covering with Con-Tact paper.

Leviticus
God's Plan for Worship

LAW

2 Samuel
David the King

HISTORY

Numbers
Wandering in the Desert

LAW

1 Samuel
The Last Judge; the First King

HISTORY

Deuteronomy
Reminders of the Law

LAW

Ruth
True Loyalty

HISTORY

Joshua
Into the Promised Land

HISTORY

Judges
Leaders of God's People

HISTORY

1 Kings
The Kingdom Divides

HISTORY

JUDAH

ISRAEL

Job
When Trouble Comes

POETRY

2 Kings
Kings and Prophets

HISTORY

Esther
A Queen's Bravery

HISTORY

1 Chronicles
David's Kingdom

HISTORY

Nehemiah
Rebuilding the Walls

HISTORY

2 Chronicles
Solomon and the Kings of Judah

HISTORY

Ezra
Return to Jerusalem

HISTORY

Psalms
Poems, Prayers and Songs
POETRY

Ezekiel
Strengthened by God
MAJOR PROPHETS

Proverbs
A Word to the Wise
POETRY

Lamentations
Prayers of Sadness
MAJOR PROPHETS

Ecclesiastes
The True Source of Wisdom
POETRY

Jeremiah
God's Future for Israel
MAJOR PROPHETS

Song of Songs
Royal Love Songs
POETRY

Isaiah
God's Plan for Salvation
MAJOR PROPHETS

To us a child is born.

Nahum

God's Justice and Love

MINOR PROPHETS

Daniel

Courage to Obey

MAJOR PROPHETS

Micah

Judgment and Hope

MINOR PROPHETS

The Lord has a case against His people.

Hosea

A Picture of God's Love

MINOR PROPHETS

Jonah

God's Mercy to All People

MINOR PROPHETS

Joel

Past Failures and Future Promises

MINOR PROPHETS

Obadiah

Israel Will Triumph

MINOR PROPHETS

Amos

Warnings Against Sin

MINOR PROPHETS

Hear this word...

Habakkuk

A Conversation with God

MINOR PROPHETS

Luke

Jesus the Son of Man

GOSPELS

Zephaniah

Sorrow and Singing

MINOR PROPHETS

Mark

Jesus the Servant

GOSPELS

Haggai*

Return and Rebuild

MINOR PROPHETS

Matthew

Jesus the King

GOSPELS

Your king is coming to you.

Zechariah*

Prepare for the King

MINOR PROPHETS

The Lord you are seeking will come.

Malachi*

Trust God for the Coming Savior

MINOR PROPHETS

John
Jesus the Son of God

GOSPELS

Philippians
Follow Jesus in Everything

LETTERS

Acts
God's Family Grows

HISTORY

Ephesians
New Life in Christ

LETTERS

Romans
God's Amazing Grace

LETTERS

Galatians
Trust Only in Jesus

LETTERS

1 Corinthians
Living as Christians

LETTERS

2 Corinthians
Stay Away from False Teachers

LETTERS

Hebrews
Jesus the Greatest Priest

LETTERS

Colossians
Christ in Charge

LETTERS

Philemon
A Servant Forgiven

LETTERS

1 Thessalonians
Jesus Our Hope

LETTERS

Titus
Encouragement for God's Leaders

LETTERS

2 Thessalonians
Jesus Will Return

LETTERS

2 Timothy
Stand Against Persecution

LETTERS

1 Timothy
Advice for Young Leaders

LETTERS

IDENTIFY AND SPELL BOOKS

Book Guess

Materials

❑ Bibles

❑ chalkboard and chalk or large sheet of paper and marker

Procedure

Lead students to play a game similar to Hangman. On chalkboard or large sheet of paper, draw blank lines for each letter of a Bible book. Students guess letters of the alphabet. Print correct letters on the appropriate blank lines. Print an incorrect letter to the side of the blank lines and print one letter of the word "Bible." Students try to guess and find the correct book in their Bibles before the word "Bible" is completed. Student who correctly guesses the word secretly chooses a different book of the Bible and draws lines for other students to guess. Continue as time permits.

Teaching Tip

If playing this game with only a specific section of the Bible, introduce the game by making a comment such as, **Today we are going to play a game to find out more about the second group of books in the Bible. These books are called the books of History because they tell the story of how God brought Abram's descendants back to their homeland many years after Abram died. The books also tell about how the people sometimes obeyed God, but more often did not obey God.** Referring to contents page in their Bibles, students take turns reading aloud the names of books of History (Joshua, Judges, Ruth, 1 Samuel, 2 Samuel, 1 Kings, 2 Kings, 1 Chronicles, 2 Chronicles, Ezra, Nehemiah, Esther). Students may also locate each book.

IDENTIFY AND SPELL BOOKS

Spell It!

Materials

❏ Bibles

❏ marker

❏ index cards

Preparation

Print the alphabet on index cards, one letter on each card. Make two sets of letter cards.
Add five blank cards to each set. (Save alphabet card sets for reuse, laminating cards if possible.)

Procedure

1. Divide the class into two teams. Give each team a set of cards to be divided as evenly as possible among team members. One student on each team opens his or her Bible to the contents page.

2. **Today we are going to play a game to help us recognize and spell the books of the Bible. Learning about the books of the Bible helps us read God's messages to us.** Call out a book of the Bible such as "Genesis." The students on each team holding the letters in the word arrange themselves to correctly spell out the word. Students use blank cards for duplicate letters. Students refer to Bible contents page to check spelling.

3. When team members think they are in the correct order, they call out the name of the book they spelled. The other team must freeze in position. If the word is spelled correctly, the team gets one point. If the book is not spelled correctly, other team unfreezes and continues to spell the book name. Then game continues on with another book. When time is called, team with the most points wins.

Teaching Tips

1. If class time is limited, play the game using only books in a certain section of the Bible (books of Law, Gospels, Letters, etc.). Introduce the game by making a comment such as, **Today we're going to play a game to help us learn the first five books of the Bible. These books are called the books of the Law because they tell about the way God began the world and the laws He gave to protect people and help them get to know Him.**

2. If you have more than 10 to 12 students, make an additional set of alphabet cards. Play the game with three teams.

PUT BOOKS IN ORDER

Book Collections

Materials

❑ Bibles

❑ Bible Book Cards (pp. 7-23) prepared as instructed (one set for every two students)

Procedure

1. **The Bible tells us what God wants us to know about Himself and the good things He wants us to do. Let's practice learning the order of the books in the Bible.** Divide class into pairs. Give each pair a set of cards to distribute evenly. Each student places his or her stack of cards facedown in front of him- or herself.

2. Simultaneously, each student places the top cards from stack faceup and says that Bible book name aloud. Students compare faceup cards. Student who played the Bible Book Card that comes later in the Bible collects both cards and adds them to the bottom of his or her stack. (For example, if one student played the card for the book of Genesis and the other student played the card for the book of Matthew, the latter student would collect both cards.)

3. Students repeat play until one student has all of the cards or time is called. Pairs reshuffle cards and play again as time allows.

Teaching Tip

Students may refer to contents page in their Bibles while playing this game.

PUT BOOKS IN ORDER

Ball Toss

Materials

❏ Bibles

❏ ball

Procedure

It is easier to find places in the Bible when we know the order of the books. Let's practice saying the books of the Bible in order. Students stand in a circle. Toss a ball to a student and say "Genesis." Student who catches the ball says "Exodus" and tosses the ball to another student. Continue tossing the ball and saying the names of the books of the Bible in order until all the books have been named. Repeat game as time permits.

Teaching Tips

1. If students are unfamiliar with books of the Bible, ask students to read aloud the names, referring to contents page in their Bibles. As students say names, print names of books in order on large sheet of paper. Display paper where all students can see it. Each student chooses a book to find in his or her Bible. After playing several rounds of the game, remove the paper.

2. For variety, limit the number of books named, gradually adding more books as students are able.

28

PUT BOOKS IN ORDER

Book Pass

Materials

❏ Bibles

❏ one set of Bible Book Cards (pp. 7-23) prepared as instructed

❏ children's music cassette/CD and player

❏ optional—construction paper strips to use as bookmarks

Procedure

1. Distribute all Bible Book Cards in mixed-up order to students. Each student finds in the Bible the books written on his or her cards. (Optional: Students use bookmarks to mark books in the Bible.)

2. As you read Bible book names from contents page in your Bible, students hold up the appropriate cards. Redistribute cards and repeat several times. **Reading the Bible helps us learn more about how God will help us love and obey Him.**

3. Collect cards. Play a game similar to Hot Potato. Select one card. Students sit in a circle. As you play music, students pass card around circle. When you stop the music, student holding card says name aloud and places it on floor. Repeat process with a different card. Student holding card when music stops places it on floor before or after the first card. Continue procedure until all books have been placed in the correct order.

Teaching Tip

Students may refer to table of contents in the front of their Bibles in order to place cards in the correct order.

PUT BOOKS IN ORDER

Go Fish!

Materials

❑ Bible Book Cards (pp. 7-23) prepared as instructed (one set for every four students)

Procedure

1. Students form groups of four. **The Bible is like a collection of books. Each book helps us learn what God is like and how He wants us to live.** Give each group a set of cards. A volunteer in each group shuffles cards and then gives each student four cards. Remaining cards are placed facedown in a stack in the middle of the group.

2. Students take turns asking other students for cards, trying to collect four Bible Book Cards in consecutive order. For example, first student asks any other student "Do you have the book of Matthew?" If student asked has the card, he or she must give it to the first student and the first student gets to ask any other student for a card.

   If student does not have the card, student answers by saying "Go fish!" and first student takes a card from the stack. If this card is the one he or she asked for, student keeps the card and discards any other card, placing it faceup next to the stack and thus creating a "fish pond." If this card is not the one he or she asked for, student places it faceup next to the stack. Next student to play may either choose a card from the "pond" or ask any student for a card.

   The game ends when one student has collected four consecutive Bible Book Cards. Student says names of cards aloud so that other students may check for accuracy.

Teaching Tip

To vary this game, provide two sets of cards for each group. Instead of collecting four consecutive Bible Book Cards, students try to collect as many pairs of consecutive book cards as possible. When a student has collected a pair, student places pair faceup and takes two cards from the stack.

PUT BOOKS IN ORDER

Line Up the Books

Materials

❑ Bibles

❑ one set of Bible Book Cards (pp. 7-23) prepared as instructed

Procedure

When we know the order of the books of the Bible, it helps us find our way around in the Bible and learn how to show God's love. Students line up. Give each student a card in the same order the books appear in the Bible. Students say the book names aloud. If time permits, students locate books in Bibles. Then at your signal, students move randomly around the room, trading cards with other students as they walk. At your signal, students put themselves in order again and say Bible book names aloud. Repeat as time permits.

Teaching Tips

1. Play additional rounds of the game by challenging students to see how fast they can arrange themselves each time.

2. To develop extra familiarity with book names, students may work together to make a set of name cards for as many books of the Bible as there are students.

Order Up!

Materials

❑ Bibles

❑ one set of Bible Book Cards (pp. 7-23) prepared as instructed

Procedure

The word "Bible" is from the Greek word that means "book," but the Bible is no ordinary book. It's a collection of 66 books. The Bible tells us what God wants us to know about Himself and His plan for us. Distribute cards to students. Invite a volunteer to come to the front of the room. Volunteer shows his or her card. Students holding names of books that come before and/or after the volunteer's stand next to volunteer in the appropriate order. Continue having students line up in this manner until all the books are in order.

Teaching Tips

1. After lining up one time, repeat the activity with students racing the clock to see how quickly they can line up in order.

2. If you have a large group, play several rounds, redistributing cards each time.

3. If your class is small, place cards on one side of the room. Students see how quickly they can race to get cards (one at a time) and put them in order.

© 1999 by Gospel Light • Permission to photocopy granted. • *The Big Book of Bible Skills*

Pick and Choose

Materials

❏ Bibles

❏ Bible Book Cards (pp. 7-23) prepared as instructed (one set for every four students)

Procedure

1. **As you get older, it's important to learn how to read and study God's Word for yourself. Today we are going to find out how well we know the order of books in the Bible.** Students form groups of four. Give one set of cards to each group. Volunteer in group shuffles cards well and gives each student 11 cards. Stack remaining cards facedown in middle of group.

2. Students organize their cards in Bible book order, referring to contents page in their Bibles. Each students tries to collect three sets of two consecutive book cards (for example—Genesis and Exodus, Matthew and Mark, Acts and Romans).

3. First player takes a card from stack. If it is a card he or she needs, player keeps the card and then discards a card, placing it faceup next to the stack. Next player may either take the discarded card or take another card from the stack. Play continues in this manner until one student has collected three sets of two consecutive books. Reshuffle and play as many rounds as time allows.

Teaching Tips

1. To vary this game, instead of collecting sets of books in consecutive order, students try to collect three sets of two cards from the same division (for example—Joshua and 1 Kings from the books of History, Psalms and Ecclesiastes from the books of Poetry, Galatians and 2 Timothy from the Letters).

2. If you have a small class, this game can be played in pairs.

3. Make a copy of "The Bible—A Library of Smaller Books" (p. 6) for each student to use in playing this game.

PUT BOOKS IN ORDER

Rapid Pass

Materials

☐ Bible Book Cards (pp. 7-23) prepared as instructed (one set for every ten students)

☐ spoons

☐ markers

☐ scraps of paper

Procedure

1. Introduce the game by telling students a way in which the Bible has helped you. **Because the Bible helps us in so many ways, it's good to learn how to find out what it says. Let's play a game to help us learn the books in order.** Students form groups of no more than five. Give each group a complete set of New Testament or Old Testament Book Cards, a spoon for each student in the group less one and a marker. Give each student a scrap of paper.

2. Students in each group sit in a circle. Place spoons and marker in the middle of the circle within easy reach of students. Volunteer in group shuffles Bible Book Cards well and then gives each student in the group four cards. Stack remaining cards facedown next to volunteer.

3. Keeping the cards facedown, volunteer begins passing cards from the stack to the student next to him or her. As students continue passing cards around the circle, they watch for cards that come before or after the cards in their hands. Students try to collect any four consecutive Bible Book Cards. If a student receives a card he or she needs, student keeps that card and passes on a card he or she does not need. Passing continues as rapidly as possible around the circle.

4. The first student to collect four consecutive Bible Book Cards quietly takes a spoon from the middle of the circle. When other students notice this action, they quickly take spoons also.

   The student who first took a spoon shows cards he or she collected to group. If the cards collected were consecutive books in the correct order, that student gets the first letter of the word "Bible" (student writes down on scrap of paper). New volunteer collects cards and shuffles well to play again. Continue play until time is called or until one student has received all the letters in the word "Bible."

Teaching Tip

To vary this game, students try to collect any four cards from the same division of the Bible. First student takes a spoon when he or she has four cards from the same division.

PUT BOOKS IN ORDER

Speed Order

Materials

❑ Bibles

❑ Bible Book Cards (pp. 7-23) prepared as instructed (one set for every four students)

Procedure

1. **The Bible is a book that we can read many times. Each time we read it we can learn more about Jesus and His love for us.** Divide class into groups of four. Give each group a set of cards to spread out facedown on floor or table. Each student chooses 10 cards.

2. At your signal, each student turns over cards he or she chose and attempts to place them in order (not necessarily consecutive). When a student thinks his or her cards are in correct order, student calls out "Freeze." Other students in group check the order of the student's cards, using Bibles when necessary. If student has correctly ordered books, collect all cards, reshuffle and play another round of the game. If student has incorrectly ordered books, other students continue play until someone calls out "Freeze" and has ordered the cards correctly. Play as many rounds as time allows.

Teaching Tip

To vary this game, use only the cards from one division of the Bible and give each student a set with which to play. First student who arranges cards in consecutive order calls out "Freeze."

PUT BOOKS IN ORDER

What's Next?

Materials

❑ Bibles

❑ Bible Book Cards (pp. 7-23) prepared as instructed (several sets)

Procedure

Over many hundreds of years God used many different writers to write the Bible. The writers were different ages and had different backgrounds, but they all wrote God's messages. Divide class into teams of two to six students each. Combine several sets of Bible Book Cards. Mix up cards and place them facedown in a stack. Teams take turns choosing cards, one at a time. If the team can tell the book of the Bible that comes after the one on the card, team gets five points. Give team an additional five points if they can also tell the name of the book that comes before the book on the card. If team must look at contents page of Bible to tell the correct names, team only receives one point. When time is called, team with the most points wins.

Teaching Tips

1. Before beginning the game, repeat names of Bible books together.
2. For each round of the game, choose new teams.

IDENTIFY BIBLE DIVISIONS—OLD OR NEW TESTAMENT DIVISIONS

Bible Book Mix-Up

Materials

❑ "The Bible—A Library of Smaller Books" (p. 6)

❑ paper

❑ photocopier

❑ chairs

Preparation

Make a copy of "The Bible—A Library of Smaller Books" for each student.

Procedure

1. Give each student a copy of "The Bible—A Library of Smaller Books." **When you hold a Bible in your hands and thumb through its pages, you see that the Bible is a collection of 66 books—a library. This collection of books is divided into two sections: the Old Testament and the New Testament. Each section is divided into several divisions. Each division has a name.** Briefly review books and divisions.

2. Lead students to play a game similar to Fruit Basket Upset. Students form a circle with chairs for each person minus one.

3. Volunteer stands in front of any student in the circle, says "New Testament" or "Old Testament" and then names one of the divisions of the books of the Bible in the testament specified. Student in chair names a book in that division. If correct, student stays in chair and volunteer repeats process with a different student seated in the circle. If student is incorrect, say "Bible Book Mix-Up." All students find new chairs. Student left without a chair becomes the new volunteer. Repeat play as time allows.

Teaching Tip

If your students are not familiar with the divisions of the Bible, limit the number of divisions used in this game.

Book Traders

Materials

❏ Bible Book Cards (pp. 7-23) prepared as instructed (one set for every three students)

Procedure

1. **The Bible is divided into parts, or divisions. Each division has books that are similar in some way. For example, the first five books of the Bible tell us about the creation of the world and how God chose a family that grew into a nation.** (Optional: Distribute Bible Book Cards in mixed-up order to students. Students sort cards by division.)

2. Divide the class into groups of three. Give each group a set of Bible Book Cards to spread out facedown on floor or table. Students each choose 12 cards. From the remaining cards, one card is placed faceup.

3. Students play a game similar to Dominoes. First player determines if he or she has a card from the same division of the Bible as the faceup card. If so, the player places the card at one end of the faceup card, as in the game of Dominoes. If player does not have a card from the same division of the Bible, he or she takes one card from the remaining cards and plays it if possible. Next player takes a turn. When all books from a division have been played, the player who played the last card starts a new division. (The single-division books of Acts and Revelation are considered wild cards and may be played at any time.) Game continues until one student has played all of his or her cards. Collect and shuffle cards to play game again.

Teaching Tips

1. Give each student a copy of "The Bible—A Library of Smaller Books" (p. 6) to use in this game.

2. As students play their cards, ask them to say aloud the names of the Bible books and the divisions to which they belong.

IDENTIFY BIBLE DIVISIONS—OLD OR NEW TESTAMENT DIVISIONS

Division Matchup

Materials

❏ Bible Book Cards (pp. 7-23) prepared as instructed (one set for every four students)

Procedure

1. Students form groups of four to play a game like Uno. Give each group a set of New Testament or Old Testament Bible Book Cards. **The books in the (Old Testament) are divided into (five) sections, or divisions. But all of these books help us learn about God.** Volunteer shuffles cards and gives each student in the group five cards. Remaining cards are stacked facedown in the middle of the group.

2. First student places a card faceup on floor or table. Next student must play a card from the same division of the Bible. If the student does not have a card from the same division, the student may play a card with the same number of letters in the book title or take a card from the stack and play it if it is of the same division. If a card is played with the same number of letters in the book title, the next student plays a card which matches the division of the new card.

3. Play continues in this manner around the circle with the exception of wild cards: (1) If the card played is either the first or last book of either the New Testament or the Old Testament, the next student must take two cards from the stack before playing a card. (2) If the card played is the first or only book in a division (for example, Romans which is the first book of Letters), the next student skips a turn. (3) If the card played is the last book of a division (for example, John which is the last book of the Gospels), the direction of play is reversed.

   When all the cards from a division of the Bible have been played, the next student plays any card to start a new division. When a student plays his or her next to last card, student must say "Divisions." If student does not say "Divisions" and another student catches him or her, student must draw another card. First student to play all cards wins the game. Shuffle cards and play again as time allows.

Teaching Tip

Provide a copy of "The Bible—A Library of Smaller Books" (p. 6) and pencils for students to use in playing this game. As books of each division of the Bible are played, students may mark off the books.

Spelling Race

Materials

- ❑ Bibles
- ❑ large sheet of paper
- ❑ marker
- ❑ tape
- ❑ optional—a copy of "The Bible—A Library of Smaller Books" (p. 6) for each student

Preparation

Draw a line down the middle of the large sheet of paper. Print "Law" at the top of one half of the paper. Print "History" at the top of the other half of the paper. Tape paper to wall.

Procedure

1. Ask volunteers to name and spell the books of the Law and History divisions of the Old Testament by using the contents page from their Bibles as a reference. (Optional: Students refer to "The Bible—A Library of Smaller Books.") As students name and spell books, you or a volunteer list books in order in the correct section of the large sheet of paper (see sketch a). **The books of Law tell how God created the world and how the nation of Israel first began. The books also tell how God freed Israel from slavery, cared for them through 40 years in a desert and gave them His laws. The books of History tell what happened when the nation of Israel entered the land God had promised them.**

2. Students sit shoulder-to-shoulder in a line, facing the paper. Volunteer stands up, calls out the name of a student and says "Law" or "History." The named student says and spells one of the books from the named category (referring to paper for book names and correct spelling) before the volunteer can do five jumping jacks as in Sketch b (or run around the line of students, hop on one foot 10 times, etc.). Repeat activity with new volunteers as time permits.

Teaching Tips

1. Play a practice round or two of the game to help students become familiar with the rules.

2. After a book has been named and spelled, mark an *X* by it on the large sheet of paper so that students will know to choose a different book in the next round.

3. For a challenge to advanced students, remove the list after playing the game once.

a.

b.

Who's Got the Beans?

Materials

- ❑ Bibles
- ❑ 10 beans for each student
- ❑ children's music cassette/CD and player

Procedure

1. Ask students to open their Bibles to the contents page. **Which books are in the Law division of the Old Testament?** (Genesis through Deuteronomy.) Volunteer reads names of the books of Law aloud. Identify the books of History and Poetry in the same way.

2. Give each student 10 beans. Group students into two equal teams: A and B. (Participate in this activity yourself if needed to balance teams.) As you play music, students move randomly around the room. When you stop the music, each student finds a partner from the opposite team. Call out either "A" or "B." Each student in the named group says the name of a book in one of the first three divisions of the Old Testament (Law, History, Poetry). Student's partner responds by saying the name of the correct division and names another book in the division. (Optional: If students are unfamiliar with books of the Bible, invite them to use contents page in Bibles to find book names.) If division named is correct, first student gives his or her partner a bean. If division named is incorrect, partner gives the first student a bean. Repeat activity as time permits. The object of the game is to have the most beans at the end of the playing period.

Teaching Tips

1. Pennies or uncooked pasta (rigatoni or wagon wheels, for example) may be used instead of beans.

2. Before playing, briefly review the first three divisions of the Old Testament: **The books of Law tell about the beginning of the world and record God's instructions to His people. The books of History tell how God led His people to a new land. These books also give us stories about their leaders. The books of Poetry are stories, songs, sayings and poems about how great and wonderful God is and how we can live in ways that please Him.** (Optional: Distribute a copy of "The Bible—A Library of Smaller Books" [p. 6] to each student.)

3. Play several practice rounds to help students become familiar with game procedures.

Prophet Talk

Materials

- ❑ Bibles
- ❑ children's music cassette/CD and player
- ❑ chalkboard
- ❑ chalk and eraser or large sheet of paper and marker

Preparation

Print the books of the Major and Minor Prophets (Isaiah through Malachi) in order on chalkboard or large sheet of paper.

Procedure

1. Students sit on the floor in a circle. Volunteer reads book names aloud from chalkboard or paper. **God sent many messengers, called prophets, to His people. These prophets spoke or wrote what God wanted His people to know. They gave many warnings to obey God and many promises about the great King and Savior who was coming! We can read these messages in the books of Prophecy. The first five books of prophecy are called the Major Prophets because these books are longer than the Minor Prophets, 12 smaller books that complete the Old Testament.**

2. Students play a game of Hot Potato, passing the eraser or marker while music plays. When music stops, say either "Major Prophets" or "Minor Prophets." Student with eraser erases a book of division you name (if using marker, student completely marks out the name).

3. Students repeat books of Major and Minor Prophets together, reciting erased or marked out books from memory. Continue playing until all books are erased or marked out and students can repeat all the books in each division from memory.

Teaching Tips

1. If you have a student who is reluctant to play the game, invite him or her to start and stop the music and name the division.

2. Sit in the circle with the students. Students enjoy getting to know their teachers while playing games together.

Mixed-Up Books

Materials

- ❏ Bibles
- ❏ index cards
- ❏ marker
- ❏ masking tape

Preparation

Print names of the books of the New Testament (Matthew through Revelation) on index cards, one name on each card. On separate cards print the names of the main divisions of New Testament books (Gospels, History, Letters, Prophecy). Make one set of book cards and one set of main division cards for every 10 students. Tear masking tape into 3-inch (7.5-cm) strips, making at least 56 strips of tape. Place strips on a table or chair where they can easily be reached and removed by students.

Procedure

1. Mix up the book cards you prepared. One at a time, hold up the cards. Students tell which division each book is part of. **All the stories in the Bible—from Adam and Eve to the very end—fit together to show us God's great plan for our world and for our own lives. In the New Testament part of the Bible, we read about the coming of the King and Savior God promised to send and all the great things that happened after God kept His promise.**

2. Divide class into at least two teams of no more than 10 students each. Teams line up in single-file lines at opposite side of classroom from where the masking-tape strips have been placed. Place a set of mixed-up book cards facedown in a pile on the floor next to the first student on each team. Tape a set of main division cards on the wall across from each team near the masking-tape strips. Leave room under each card for book cards to be taped (see sketch).

3. At your signal, the first student in each line takes a book card, runs to the division cards, grabs a piece of tape and tapes the book card to the wall, below the correct division card. Student returns to his or her team and tags the next student in line. Play continues until all teams have taped cards onto the wall under the correct category.

Teaching Tip

If your students are not familiar with the New Testament divisions, give each team a copy of "The Bible—A Library of Smaller Books" (p. 6) to use in playing the game.

IDENTIFY BIBLE DIVISIONS—NEW TESTAMENT

Walk and Talk

Materials

❏ Bibles

❏ butcher paper

❏ tape

❏ markers

❏ children's music cassette/CD and player

Preparation

Cover tabletop with butcher paper. Draw lines to divide the paper into sections, one section for each student. Print names of divisions of the New Testament (Gospels, History, Letters, Prophecy) in separate sections, repeating divisions as needed.

Procedure

1. **The New Testament tells that God's promise to send a Savior came true and that God's keeping of His promise makes a difference in our world.** Students walk around table with Bibles while you play music. When you stop the music, each student puts a hand on one section on the paper and then refers to the contents page in his or her Bible to find a book in the New Testament from the division named in the section. After all students have found books in their Bibles, each student says the division and book names aloud. Repeat several times.

2. Turn over the butcher paper and tape it to tabletop. Students walk around table while you play song. When you stop the music, call out a New Testament division. Each student writes the name of a book in the division. Play several rounds of the game.

Teaching Tips

1. Introduce the New Testament sections by explaining, **The word "gospel" means "good news." The four Gospels tell the good news about Jesus. The History book, Acts, tells what God's Holy Spirit did through people who took the good news about Jesus to the rest of world. The next section of the New Testament is Letters. The Letters were written to encourage people to live as Christians. The last section is Prophecy. This book, Revelation, tells about the future time when Jesus will come back to earth, and everyone will know He really is the King of kings.**

2. Give each student a copy of "The Bible—A Library of Smaller Books" (p. 6) to use in playing this game.

IDENTIFY KEY PHRASES

Content Concentration

Materials

❑ Bibles

❑ Bible Book Cards (pp. 7-23) prepared as instructed
(two sets for each group of six to eight students)

Procedure

1. One at a time, show Bible Book Cards. (Optional: Students locate books in Bibles.) **The phrases on these cards help us remember what each book is about. As we read the stories in each of these books, we learn reasons to honor and praise God.**

2. Divide class into groups of six to eight. Give each group two sets of cards you prepared. Students mix up cards and spread them facedown in rows on the floor. Students take turns turning over two cards at a time. If the cards match, student keeps the cards. If the cards do not match, he or she turns the cards facedown again. Play continues until all the cards are matched. Player with the most pairs wins. Repeat activity as time permits.

Teaching Tip

Limit the number of cards used to one or more sections of the Bible.

IDENTIFY KEY PHRASES

Get a Clue!

Materials

❏ Bibles

❏ Bible Book Cards (pp. 7-23) prepared as instructed (one set for every four students)

Procedure

1. One at a time, show the Bible Book Cards and read the phrases aloud. (Optional: Students locate books in Bibles.) **The phrases will help you remember the main ideas or events in the books of the Bible.**

2. Divide the class into groups of four. Give each group a set of cards. Volunteer shuffles and stacks cards facedown in the middle of the group.

3. First player in each group takes a card from the stack and reads aloud the key phrase written on the card. Other students in group tell which Bible book the key phrase describes. Student who first names the correct book gets the card. If no student guesses the correct book after each student in group has made one guess, player reveals the correct answer and keeps the card. Next player takes a turn.

4. When all cards in the stack are gone, each student counts up the number of cards he or she has collected. Student with the most cards wins.

Teaching Tips

1. If students are unfamiliar with the key phrases and divisions of the Bible, use only the Bible Book Cards from two or three divisions.

2. If time permits, allow students time to practice matching book names and phrases.

IDENTIFY KEY PHRASES

Match Up

Materials

❏ Bibles

❏ index cards

❏ marker

Preparation

Print names of the books of the Bible on index cards, one name on each card. On separate cards print phrases that describe the books (refer to pp. 7-23).

Procedure

1. One at a time, show the phrase cards you prepared, matching each one with the appropriate Bible book. **These phrases help us remember what each book is about.** Ask volunteers to tell something they know about different books.

2. Divide class into two groups. Give one group cards with book names. Give the other group cards with key phrases. (Students hold more than one card if needed.) Groups stand on opposite sides of the room. At your signal, students move around the room to find cards that match the cards they are holding. Students locate books in their Bibles and then place matched cards in a pile. Continue until all the cards are matched.

Teaching Tips

1. Provide a set of Bible Book Cards (pp. 7-23, prepared as instructed) for students to refer to during the activity.

2. If students are having a difficult time remembering key phrases for all the books of the Bible, play the game with just a few books and key phrases at a time.

Name That Letter!

Materials

❑ Bibles

❑ index cards

❑ marker

❑ large sheet of paper and marker or chalkboard and chalk

❑ optional—individually wrapped candies or other small rewards

Preparation

Print names of the books of the Bible on index cards, one name on each card. On separate cards print phrases that describe the books (refer to pp. 7-23).

Procedure

1. Distribute the Bible book and phrase cards you prepared, saying the names of the books and reading the phrases aloud. Students practice matching books and phrases several times. **These phrases help us remember what we learn in each book.**

2. Draw one blank line for each letter of one of the key phrases on paper or chalkboard. Students guess letters until they are able to guess the phrase and tell the book that goes with it. (Optional: Draw a star under several of the blank lines. Each time a student guesses a letter that belongs on one of those lines, he or she receives a reward.) Continue with the other key phrases as time permits.

Command Talk

Materials

❏ Bibles

❏ index cards

❏ marker

Preparation

Print these references on index cards, one reference on each card: Exodus 20:3; 20:8; 20:12; Deuteronomy 4:39; 6:5; Joshua 1:8; 23:6; 2 Chronicles 15:7.

Procedure

1. **There are several different kinds of verses in the Bible. Commands are verses that tell us things that God wants us to do, say or remember.**

2. Play a game to list commands in the Bible. Place verse cards facedown on a table. Volunteer chooses a card, finds the verse in his or her Bible and reads it aloud, leaving out two or three words. Other students attempt to guess the missing words.

3. Student who correctly guesses the last word tells a way to obey the command in the verse and then chooses another card to find and read the next verse. Continue with other verses as time permits or until each student has had a turn to locate a verse in the Bible.

Teaching Tips

1. Before beginning the game, repeat names of the first 14 Bible books (Genesis through 2 Chronicles) together.

2. Clarify the chapter and verse references as needed. Explain, **The name of each Bible book is printed at the top of each page. The big numbers on each page are the chapter numbers. The smaller numbers are the verses. Some Bibles also print the chapter and verse numbers at the top of each page.**

Hands on Leaders

Materials

- ❏ Bibles
- ❏ butcher paper
- ❏ tape
- ❏ marker
- ❏ children's music cassette/CD and player

Preparation

Cover tabletop with butcher paper. Draw lines to divide the paper into sections, one section for each student. Print one of these Bible references in each section: 1 Samuel 10:1; 16:13; 1 Kings 17:2-4; 2 Kings 18:5; 2 Chronicles 5:1; 34:1,2; Nehemiah 8:2,3. Make one table for each group of six to seven students.

Procedure

Students walk around table while you play music. When you stop the music, each student puts hand on one section and finds the Bible reference printed in the section. Invite students to read the verses aloud and tell the names of Bible characters they have read about and in which book of the Bible the characters are written about. As characters are identified say, **These are the people God chose to be the leaders of His people. We can read true stories about what these people did in the books of History.**

Teaching Tip

Provide several Bible dictionaries (or encyclopedias). Students find names of leaders in dictionaries (or encyclopedias) and tell information about the leaders.

Leader Hunt

Materials

☐ Bibles

☐ 16 slips of paper

☐ basket or other container

☐ pencils

☐ a 3-foot (.9-m) butcher-paper square for each student

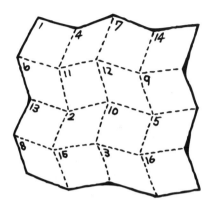

Preparation

Number slips of paper from 1 to 16 and place them in the basket or other container.

Procedure

1. **The first 17 books of the Bible tell us about the first people God made and the people who became leaders of God's people. Let's find and read about some of the people who were God's leaders.** Each student folds a butcher-paper square in half four times and then unfolds paper to reveal 16 squares. Student numbers the squares randomly from 1 to 16, writing the numbers small in the corners of squares (see sketch).

2. Play a game similar to Bingo. Choose a number from the container and read the number aloud, designating this square as the one to be used for the first round. Then say, **Genesis 2:20.** Each student finds and reads the verse in his or her Bible, identifying the name(s) of the Bible character(s) mentioned in the verse. Student writes the name(s) of the Bible character(s) in the designated square. Continue activity, choosing new numbers for the following references: Genesis 3:20; 6:8; 12:1; 21:3; 24:15; 25:25; 25:26; 37:3; Exodus 2:10; Joshua 1:1; Judges 4:4; 6:12; 13:24; Ruth 1:16; 1 Samuel 3:10. After each Bible character is named, invite students to tell information about the character. Play continues until one student has written names in four squares in a row vertically, horizontally or diagonally.

Teaching Tips

1. Repeat game as time permits, using reverse sides of butcher-paper squares or folding new papers.

2. If you have a large class, form groups of four or five students each and give each group its own butcher-paper square.

3. To talk with students about how to find verses in the Bible say, **The Bible is made up of 66 books. Each book is divided into chapters (except a couple, which are really short), and each chapter is divided into many verses. When we want to find something in the Bible, we can look up its reference just like an address. The reference Genesis 1:1, for example, means the book of Genesis, chapter 1, verse 1.**

4. Before playing the game, say names of the first 17 books of the Bible (Genesis through Esther) in order and display a list of the first 17 books of the Bible in order for students to refer to.

Love and Obey Verses

Materials

❑ Bibles

❑ large sheet of paper and marker or chalkboard and chalk

Preparation

Print these references on paper or chalkboard, drawing blank lines for all but two to four letters in each book name: Exodus 19:5; Leviticus 18:4; Deuteronomy 30:16; Joshua 1:8; 1 Samuel 15:22; 1 Kings 8:61; 2 Chronicles 34:31; Psalm 119:34.

Procedure

1. Display references you prepared. Volunteers try to identify Bible book names, guessing letters as needed.

2. **These Bible books are found in the first three sections of the Old Testament. What are these sections called?** (The books of Law, History and Poetry.) **The verses listed here tell us how we show love for God by obeying Him.**

3. Each student chooses a verse reference to locate and read aloud. More than one student may locate each reference.

Teaching Tips

1. If your students are not familiar with the Bible book names, include more than two or three letters in each Bible book name.

2. Add interest to the game by assigning a point value to each blank line. When a student guesses the missing letter, he or she receives the appropriate number of points. At the end of the game, give a small prize to the student with the most points.

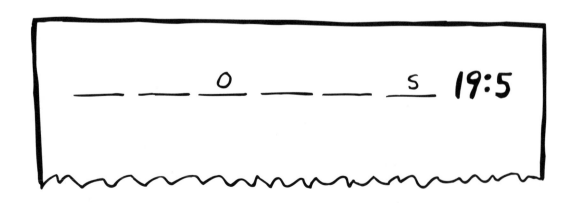

LOCATE REFERENCES—OLD TESTAMENT

Power Search

Materials

❑ Bibles

❑ large sheet of paper and marker or chalkboard and chalk

Preparation

Print these Bible references in random order on paper or chalkboard, leaving room to write next to each reference: Genesis 1:31; 28:15; Deuteronomy 4:31; Joshua 1:9; 2 Samuel 22:31; Job 37:5,6; Psalm 18:2; 19:1; 103:2,3; 147:7-9.

Procedure

1. **God's power is written about in many books of the Bible.** Show references you prepared. **Each of these Bible verses describes something God does because of His power. Learning about God's power reminds us to be confident when we're feeling afraid. The verses are all in the first three sections of the Bible. What are these sections called?** (The books of Law, History and Poetry.)

2. Group students into pairs or trios. Assign each pair or trio a Bible reference. Group finds and reads assigned verse, choosing a key word from the verse. **A key word in a Bible verse is a word that helps you understand why the verse is important.**

3. Play a game similar to Hangman. Volunteer from each group takes a turn to draw blank lines (one line for each letter of the key word) near the appropriate reference on the paper or chalkboard. Other students guess letters of the alphabet until the key word has been identified. Group reads verse from Bible.

Teaching Tips

1. Repeat the books of Law, History and Poetry (Genesis through Song of Songs) with students before dividing class into pairs or trios. You may also suggest students refer to contents page in front of Bibles if they need help locating a specific Bible book.

2. If time permits, ask all students to find and read the Bible verse after the key word has been identified.

Praise Puzzles

Materials

- ❏ Bibles
- ❏ index cards
- ❏ marker
- ❏ scissors

Preparation

Print each of the following references on a separate index card: Exodus 15:2; 18:10; Deuteronomy 10:21; 2 Samuel 7:22; 1 Kings 8:23; Nehemiah 9:6; Psalm 18:31; 148:1-3. Cut each card into two puzzle pieces as shown in sketch.

Procedure

1. Count the number of students present. Ask students to close eyes while you hide puzzle pieces, making sure to hide one piece for each student. (Participate in this activity yourself if needed to create an even number of players.) Each student finds a hidden puzzle piece and then finds the student whose puzzle piece fits with his or hers. Pairs locate the Bible verse in their Bibles.

2. Invite students to read their Bible verses aloud. **What is similar about all these verses?** (They are prayers of praise to God.) **What sections of the Bible are these verses found in?** (Books of Law, History and Poetry.) Repeat activity as time permits, hiding different puzzle pieces or hiding the same pieces again.

Teaching Tip

If you will have more than 16 students in your class, make more than one card for each reference.

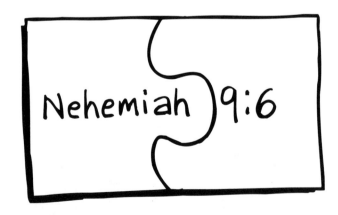

Promise Search

Materials

❏ Bibles

❏ large sheet of paper and marker or chalkboard and chalk

Preparation

Print these Bible references in random order on paper or chalkboard, leaving room to write near each reference: Genesis 8:22; Exodus 15:13; 20:12; Deuteronomy 4:29; Joshua 1:9; 1 Samuel 26:23; 2 Chronicles 7:14; Nehemiah 9:31.

Procedure

1. **God's promises are written about in the Bible.** Show paper or chalkboard you prepared. **Each of these Bible verses tells about a promise God makes or something we can depend on God to do. The verses are all in the first two sections of the Bible. What are these sections called?** (The books of Law and History.)

2. Group students in pairs or trios. Assign each pair or trio a Bible reference you prepared. Group finds and reads assigned verse, choosing a key word from the verse. To help groups choose key words, ask, **Which word is most important in this verse? Why? Which word helps you understand the main idea of the verse?**

3. Volunteer from each group takes a turn to say a word that rhymes with the key word. Other students try to guess the key word. Volunteer says additional rhyming words as needed. When the key word has been identified, group reads verse from Bible.

Teaching Tips

1. Repeat the books of Law and History (Genesis through Esther) with students before dividing class into pairs or trios. You may also suggest students refer to contents page in front of Bibles if they need help locating a specific Bible book.

2. If time permits, ask all students to find and read the Bible verse after the key word has been identified.

Discover a Story

Materials

❏ Bibles

❏ index cards

❏ marker

❏ beanbag

❏ pencils

Preparation

On separate index cards, print these Bible references: Matthew 7:24-27; 13:1-9; 18:12-14; Luke 10:30-37; 15:3-7; 15:8-10. Make a card for each student, repeating references as needed or adding references to other parables.

Procedure

1. **Jesus told many stories to teach His disciples about God. Let's find out about some of these stories.**

2. Place index cards facedown in rows on floor. Each student takes a turn to stand 5 to 6 feet (1.5 to 1.8 m) away from the index cards and toss the beanbag onto the cards. Student picks up the card on which the beanbag lands. When all students have picked up a card, students find and read the references on their cards. Each student then draws a picture of something in the story on the back of the index card.

3. Lead students in showing their pictures and discussing the parables by asking, **What did Jesus want His listeners to learn from this story?** Repeat game, reusing cards and adding different pictures of items or people in stories to cards as time permits.

Teaching Tips

1. To help students become familiar with the books of the New Testament (Matthew through Revelation), repeat the names of the books with students.

2. This game may also be played at a table, tossing a coin instead of a beanbag.

3. Make a set of cards and provide a beanbag for each group of six to eight students.

Easter Story Comparison

Materials

- ❏ Bibles
- ❏ 16 slips of paper
- ❏ basket or other container
- ❏ pencils
- ❏ a 3-foot (.9-m) butcher-paper square for each pair or trio of students

Preparation

Number slips of paper from 1 to 16 and place them in the basket or other container.

Procedure

1. **What are the names of the four Gospels?** (Matthew, Mark, Luke, John.) **Each of the Gospels tells about how Jesus died and came back to life again, but each one tells the information a little differently. Let's find and read the different information in the Gospels so that we can hear the whole story.**

2. Lead students in playing a game similar to Bingo. Divide class into pairs or trios. Give each group a butcher-paper square. Students fold butcher-paper squares in half four times and then unfold paper to reveal 16 squares. Students number the squares randomly from 1 to 16, writing small numbers in the corners of squares (see sketch).

3. Choose a number from the container and read the number aloud, designating this square as the one to be used for the first round. Then say, **Luke 24:1**. Each student finds and reads the verse in his or her Bible, identifying information about the Easter story mentioned in the verse. Volunteer in each pair or trio writes one piece of information (person, place, time, object, etc.) in the designated square.

   Continue process, choosing new numbers for the following references: Matthew 28:1; 28:2; 28:5,6; 28:9,10; Mark 16:1; 16:2,3; 16:4; 16:9-11; 16:12,13; Luke 24:3; 24:4; 24:12; 24:13-16; John 20:11-13; 20:14-16. Play continues until information has been written in four squares in a row vertically, horizontally or diagonally.

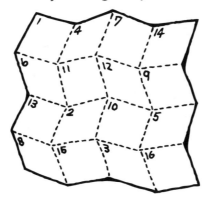

Good News Fill-In

Materials

❑ Bibles

❑ index cards

❑ marker

Preparation

Print these references on separate index cards, one reference on each card: Matthew 1:21; 8:2; 16:15,16; Mark 10:45; Luke 2:11; 5:31,32; John 1:29; 3:16.

Procedure

What are the names of the books in the Bible that tell the good news about Jesus? (The Gospels: Matthew, Mark, Luke, John.) Play a game to find verses in the Gospels which tell the good news about Jesus. Distribute verse cards to volunteers. Students find verses in their Bibles. First student reads verse(s) aloud, leaving out one or two important words. Student gives several clues to the missing words. Other students attempt to guess the missing words. Continue with other volunteers and verses as time permits or until each student has had a turn to locate a verse in the Bible.

Teaching Tips

1. Before beginning the game, repeat names of New Testament books (Matthew through Revelation) together.

2. Clarify the chapter and verse references as needed. Explain, **The name of each Bible book is printed at the top of each page. The big numbers on each page are the chapter numbers. The smaller numbers are the verses. Some Bibles also print the chapter and verse numbers at the top of each page.**

58

LOCATE REFERENCES—NEW TESTAMENT

Gospel Puzzles

Materials

❑ Bibles

❑ index cards

❑ blue, red, purple and green markers

❑ scissors

Preparation

Print in the colors indicated the following references on separate index cards:

   blue—Matthew 21:1-3; Mark 11:1-3; Luke 19:28-31

   red—Mark 11:4-6; Luke 19:32-34

   purple—Matthew 21:9; Mark 11:9,10; Luke 19:38; John 12:13

   green—Matthew 21:15,16; Mark 11:18; Luke 19:39,40

Cut each card into two puzzle pieces as shown in sketch.

Procedure

1. Count the number of students present. Ask students to close eyes while you hide puzzle pieces, making sure to hide one piece for each student. (Use all the cards of one color before using another color.) Participate in this activity yourself if needed to create an even number of players. Each student finds a hidden puzzle piece and then finds the student holding the matching puzzle piece. Students read the Bible passage in their Bibles.

2. Invite students to read their Bible passages aloud. **In what section of the Bible are these verses found? (The Gospels.) What is similar about all the (blue) passages? (They tell what Jesus told His disciples to do.) How are the (blue) passages different from each other? Each of the Gospels tells the story of Jesus' life in a slightly different way. The people who wrote these books included different information about the same events. When we read the different accounts of each event, we get a better idea of everything that happened.**

3. Repeat activity as time permits, hiding different puzzle pieces or hiding the same pieces again.

Life of Jesus Time Line

Materials

☐ Bibles

☐ index cards

☐ marker

☐ masking tape

Preparation

Print the following references on index cards, one reference on each card: Luke 2:6,7; 2:42,43; 3:21,22; 4:1,2; 4:38,39; 7:11-17; 19:35-37; 19:45,46; 22:52,54; 23:33,34; 24:1-3; 24:34,35; 24:50,51. Make a 5-foot (1.5-m) line on a wall with masking tape.

Procedure

1. **Time lines show the order of things that have happened. The book of Luke is one of the books that tells events that happened in Jesus' life. Let's see if we can find some events in Jesus' life from the book of Luke and put them in order on a time line.**

2. Distribute cards to students, one card to each student. Students find references in their Bibles and write on the backs of their index cards a sentence about the event(s) described in their verses. Students take turns reading sentences aloud. **Which of these events happened first in Jesus' life?** Guide students to determine the event that happened earliest in Jesus' life. Student with that card tapes card at the beginning of the masking-tape line. Continue until all the cards are in order, referring to chapter and verse numbers on the backs of the cards.

Teaching Tips

1. Remove masking tape immediately after the activity so that it will not damage walls. (Masking-tape line may also be made on butcher paper rather than on the wall.)

2. If you have more than 13 students, group students in pairs or small groups to find references. If you have fewer than 13 students, give some students more than one card.

Name That Disciple

Materials

- ❏ Bibles
- ❏ index cards
- ❏ marker
- ❏ several Bible dictionaries (at least one for every four students)

Preparation

Print names of the 12 disciples (Simon Peter, Andrew, James, John, Matthew, Philip, Bartholomew, Thomas, James the son of Alphaeus, Thaddaeus, Simon the Zealot and Judas Iscariot) on index cards, one name on each card. Make at least one card for each student, repeating names as needed.

Procedure

1. **Jesus traveled with and taught a group of 12 men. What were these men called?** (Disciples, or apostles.) **What are the names of Jesus' 12 disciples?** Students read disciples' names in Matthew 10:2-4. **These men saw Jesus do many wonderful things. Let's see if we can find out more about these people.**

2. Place cards you prepared in a stack. Divide class into pairs. First pair faces each other and plays Rock, Paper, Scissors. Winner of the round takes a card. Continue with other pairs until each pair has a card. Students in each pair find the disciple's name in a Bible dictionary and find one or more facts about the disciple. Each pair takes a turn to tell facts to the class.

Teaching Tips

1. Instead of preparing cards ahead of time, students make cards, finding Matthew 10:2-4 in their Bibles and taking turns writing names on separate index cards.

2. The goal of this activity is to help students become familiar with using a Bible dictionary as a Bible study tool. You may also wish to provide a children's Bible encyclopedia or a concordance for students to use in finding more information about disciples.

People Scrabble

Materials

☐ Bibles

☐ graph paper

☐ pencil

☐ index cards

Preparation

On a sheet of graph paper, outline a grid with at least 20 vertical and horizontal columns. On separate index cards, print these Bible references: Matthew 1:18; 2:1; 2:13; Luke 1:5; 1:19; 1:26,27; 2:1; 2:8; 2:10; 2:46.

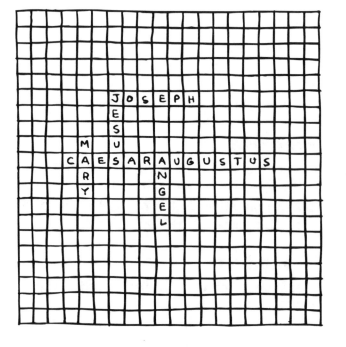

Procedure

1. **What do you think are some of the most famous stories in the Bible?** Volunteers tell opinions (stories of creation, Noah's ark, David and Goliath, Jesus' miracles, etc.). **Why are these stories so famous?** (People like hearing them. The stories are exciting. They tell about important things.) **Some stories in the Bible are so important they are written about more than once. The events that happened during the time when Jesus was born and grew as a child are described in several different books of the Bible. What are the books called which tell the stories of Jesus' life?** (The Gospels: Matthew, Mark, Luke, John.) **Let's practice finding references in these books.**

2. Group students into pairs or trios. Place index cards facedown near grid. At your signal each group chooses an index card and finds the Bible reference printed on the card. First group to find reference reads verse(s) to discover one or more names of people. Group prints name(s) of person on graph paper, trying to connect the names together as in Scrabble (see sketch).

3. If a group is unable to connect a name, group selects another Bible reference, trying to add the first name to the grid later on. Groups continue taking turns until all references have been read or until there is no more space to add names to the grid. (Names may be written more than once.) **What are some of the events these names remind you of?** Volunteers answer.

Teaching Tip

If you do not have any graph paper, draw grid on large sheet of paper.

BIBLE MEMORY

Around the Verse

Materials

- ❏ Bible
- ❏ large sheet of paper
- ❏ marker
- ❏ small unbreakable object
- ❏ individually wrapped candies
- ❏ children's music cassette/CD and player

Preparation

Print the words of a Bible memory verse on large sheet of paper, dividing the verse into seven or eight parts.

Procedure

1. Students sit in a circle around large sheet of paper you prepared. Students play a game similar to Hot Potato. As you play music, students pass object around the circle. When the music stops, the student holding the object says the first part of the verse. Student on his or her right says the next part of the verse.

2. Continue around the circle until the entire verse has been quoted. Last student places a piece of candy on a word on the paper. Repeat activity until all the words are covered or as time permits.

3. Divide candy so that each student has at least one piece, and eat candy together.

Teaching Tip

If you have students who cannot eat candy, be sure to provide other snacks or treats such as crackers, raisins, stickers, etc.

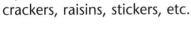

BIBLE MEMORY

Back-to-Back Attack

Materials

❏ Bibles

❏ index cards

❏ marker

Preparation

Print the words of a Bible memory verse and its reference on index cards, one word or phrase on each card. Make enough cards so that there is at least one card for every two students. Place cards faceup on the floor around the room, making sure the cards are a safe distance away from furniture or walls.

Procedure

1. Divide class into pairs of students of similar height, if possible. Students stand back-to-back with partners, linking elbows (see sketch).

2. Pairs practice sitting down and standing up with their arms linked and staying in the back-to-back position. After practice, pairs walk in the linked position to a card on the floor, sit down together to pick it up and bring it to a designated place in the room.

3. When all cards have been collected, students unlink arms and find verse in their Bibles. All students work together to place cards in verse order. Read verse aloud.

Balloon Bop

Materials

☐ Bible

☐ balloons

☐ masking tape

☐ large sheet of paper

☐ marker

Preparation

Blow up and tie balloons (one for each pair of students). Use masking tape to make a long line on the floor in an open area. Print a Bible memory verse on large sheet of paper.

Procedure

Divide class into pairs. Pairs stand on opposite sides of the masking-tape line. Give one student in each pair an inflated balloon. Pairs attempt to tap the balloon back and forth across the line to each other, repeating the words of the Bible memory verse in order.

Table Option

Instead of tapping balloons back and forth, students in each pair sit on opposite sides of a table and slide coins across table to each other.

Teaching Tips

1. As a variation, have students stand in a circle and attempt to tap the balloon around the circle, repeating the words of the verse in order.

2. Prepare balloons ahead of time and put in large plastic garbage bag to bring to class.

BIBLE MEMORY

Balloon Release

Materials

- ❏ Bibles
- ❏ large sheet of paper
- ❏ permanent markers
- ❏ index cards
- ❏ tape
- ❏ balloons

Preparation

Print the words of a Bible memory verse and its reference on a large sheet of paper. Lightly tape an index card over each word. Display paper on wall in your classroom.

Procedure

1. Give each student a balloon. Students write their initials on balloons. Students blow up balloons and pinch openings closed so that air does not escape.

2. Students stand in a line at least 5 feet (1.5 m) away from paper you prepared. At your signal students release balloons. One or two students whose balloons land the closest to the paper you prepared each remove one of the index cards. Students attempt to say verse, guessing words that are still covered with cards.

3. Students find and blow up their balloons again, continuing to release balloons and remove cards until all but two or three of the cards have been removed. **What do you think the last words are?** Students guess the words under the remaining cards before finding the verse in their Bibles. Remove the cards and say verse together.

BIBLE MEMORY

Ball Toss

Materials

❑ Bibles

❑ index cards

❑ marker

❑ container (trash can or large basket)

❑ scratch paper

Preparation

Print the words of a Bible memory verse and its reference on index cards, one to three words on each card.

Procedure

1. Students line up approximately 3 feet (.9 m) from container. Mix up the verse cards you prepared and place them facedown in a stack near students. First student crumples scratch paper to make a paper ball and attempts to toss it into container. If the paper ball goes into the container, the student takes a card from stack. Students continue taking turns tossing paper balls until all the cards have been collected.

2. Students find and read the Bible memory verse in their Bibles, noting the words that come before and after the words on their cards. At your signal, students work together to put cards in order. Students read verse together.

3. Mix up cards and play game again. This time students put verse in order without looking in their Bibles.

Teaching Tip

If you have a large class, make additional sets of cards and divide class into groups of six to eight students each.

BIBLE MEMORY

Believe It or Not!

Materials

❑ Bible

❑ two sheets of paper

❑ 10 index cards

❑ marker

Preparation

Print the words of a Bible memory verse on both sheets of paper, leaving blank underlined spaces for five key words. Print each of these words on separate index cards, making two sets.

Procedure

1. Play a game similar to Go Fish. Divide class into two teams, with at least two players on each team. Give each team a sheet of paper and one set of index cards. Cards are distributed among the players on each team.

2. Volunteer from first team tries to identify who on the other team has one of the missing words by saying "I believe Jana has the word (love)." If the named player has the card, he or she gives it to the first team who then places the card on the appropriate line on its sheet of paper and takes another turn. If the named player does not have the card, volunteer from the other team takes a turn.

3. Continue procedure with teams taking turns until each team has collected all the cards needed for its sheet of paper. Read verse aloud.

BIBLE MEMORY

Burst Your Bubble

Materials

❏ Bibles

❏ slips of paper

❏ marker

❏ balloons

❏ large plastic garbage bag

Preparation

Print one to three words of a Bible memory verse and its reference on separate slips of paper, making one paper for each student. (Repeat key words of verse if needed.) Blow up balloons, inserting one rolled slip of paper into each balloon before tying. Put balloons in garbage bag to bring to class.

Procedure

1. Students choose balloons, pop them and find papers inside.
2. Students read the verse in their Bibles and arrange slips of paper in verse order.

BIBLE MEMORY

Charades

Materials

❏ Bibles

❏ index cards

❏ marker

Preparation

Find a Bible memory verse which includes several words which are easily pantomimed. Print each of these words on a separate card.

Procedure

1. Students play a game similar to Charades. Volunteer chooses a card and pantomimes his or her word until other students guess it. Continue with other volunteers until all the words have been guessed.

2. Tell students the reference for the verse. Students find verse in their Bibles and read it aloud.

Concentration

Materials

❏ Bibles

❏ index cards

❏ marker

Preparation

Print the words of a Bible memory verse and its reference on index cards, two or three words on each card. Make two identical sets.

Procedure

1. Play a game of Concentration. Mix up both sets of cards. Place cards facedown in rows. Students take turns turning over two cards at a time to see if they match. If they match, students keep the cards. If they do not match, students turn cards facedown again. Play until all cards have been collected.

2. Students work together to put both sets of cards in verse order, referring to their Bibles for help.

BIBLE MEMORY

Group Fill-in-the-Blanks

Materials

❏ Bible

❏ index cards

❏ marker

❏ pencils

❏ paper

Preparation

Print each word of a Bible memory verse on a separate index card. Number the cards in verse order, writing numbers on the backs of the cards.

Procedure

1. Give each student a sheet of paper and a pencil. Students draw horizontal lines on their papers and number the lines in order, making a line for each word in the verse and leaving enough room to write a word on each line. Pass out index cards. Depending on the number of students in your group, some students may have more than one card.

2. Students move around the room asking other students what numbers and words are on their cards and recording words on the numbered lines on their papers. When finished, students read verse aloud together.

Hidden Words

Materials

- ❏ Bibles
- ❏ index cards
- ❏ marker
- ❏ scissors

Preparation

Print the words of a Bible memory verse and its reference on index cards, one word on each card. Cut cards in half. Hide the pieces in the classroom for students to find.

Procedure

As students arrive, invite them to search for pieces of the verse cards. Students place cards together to find the words of the verse. Students find verse in their Bibles and put cards in order. Students read verse together.

Table Option

Instead of hiding words, distribute them in mixed-up order.

BIBLE MEMORY

Last Word

Materials

❏ Bibles

❏ index cards

❏ marker

Preparation

Print the words of a Bible memory verse and its reference without any punctuation on separate index cards.

Procedure

1. Mix words you prepared and place them faceup on floor or table. Students look at words and predict which word they think is the last word of the verse. Then distribute equally to each student.

2. Students locate Bible memory verse in their Bibles and refer to the verse as they work together to put pieces in order.

BIBLE MEMORY

Listen Up!

Materials

❑ Bible

❑ two sheets of paper

❑ marker

❑ blindfold

Preparation

Divide the words of a Bible memory verse into two parts. Print each part on a separate sheet of paper.

Procedure

1. Play a game like Marco Polo. Ask a volunteer to stand on one side of the room. Blindfold the volunteer. Remaining students stand on other side of classroom. Give the papers you prepared to two students who quietly position themselves at random in the room.

2. At your signal, student with the first part of the verse calls out the words several times, pausing between each repetition. Blindfolded volunteer moves toward the student by listening to his or her voice. After finding first student, volunteer repeats the process to find the second student.

3. Continue with other volunteers and students as time permits.

Table Option

Print verse on cards, one word on each card. Spread out cards in mixed-up order on table. Blindfolded student puts verse cards in order, listening to instructions from other students.

Memory Add-On

Materials

❏ Bibles

Procedure

1. Read the words of a Bible memory verse aloud, including its reference. Ask students to find the verse in their Bibles and repeat it together several times.

2. Play a memory game. Students sit in a circle on the floor or around a table. First student says first word of verse. Second student says first and second words, and so on until the entire verse has been quoted. (Students check verse order in their Bibles.) Repeat as time and interest allow.

BIBLE MEMORY

Memory Pass

Materials

❏ Bibles

❏ chalkboard, chalk and eraser or large sheet of paper and marker

❏ children's music cassette/CD and player

Preparation

Print the words of a Bible memory verse and its reference on chalkboard or paper.

Procedure

1. Students sit in a circle on the floor or around a table. Students read verse aloud and then play a game of Hot Potato, passing the eraser or marker as music is played. When music stops, student with eraser erases a word or two from the verse or if using marker, completely marks out the word. Students say verse together, reciting erased or marked-out words from memory.

2. Continue playing until all words are erased or marked out. Students find verse in their Bibles.

Memory Pictures

Materials

- ❏ Bibles
- ❏ index cards
- ❏ marker
- ❏ large sheets of paper

Preparation

Choose a Bible memory verse which includes several words which are easily illustrated. Print each of these words on a separate index card.

Procedure

1. Students play a game similar to Pictionary. Volunteer chooses a card and draws pictures on large sheet of paper to give clues about the word on the card. Other students guess the word.
2. Students take turns continuing to draw pictures until all the words have been guessed.
3. Tell students the reference of the verse. Students find verse in their Bibles. Volunteer reads verse aloud.

Missing Words

Materials

- ❏ Bibles
- ❏ large sheet of paper
- ❏ marker
- ❏ index cards
- ❏ tape

Preparation

Print the words of a Bible memory verse and its reference on large sheet of paper, drawing blank lines for six to eight key words. Write each key word on a separate index card.

Procedure

1. Place index cards and paper you prepared faceup on table or floor. Students take turns choosing index cards to place in blanks on large sheet of paper. When taking his or her turn, student may ask classmates if they agree or disagree with the placement of a card by a previous student. Student may switch or remove a card only if a majority of the class disagrees with the card's placement.

2. After students think they have correctly completed the verse, students check verse in Bibles and correct placement of cards as needed. Students tape cards in place.

Out of Order

Materials

❏ Bibles

❏ large index cards

❏ marker

Preparation

Print the words of a Bible memory verse and its reference on large index cards, one word on each card. Make one set of cards for each group of up to six students.

Procedure

1. Arrange verse cards so that the verse makes sense but has one or two words out of order. Students read verse. Then students find and read the verse in their Bibles and arrange cards in the correct order.

2. Divide class into groups of up to six. Give each group a set of verse cards. Students take turns arranging cards with one or more words out of order, letting other students in the group arrange words in the correct order.

Puzzling Words

Materials

- ❏ Bibles
- ❏ large index cards
- ❏ red and green markers
- ❏ scissors
- ❏ tape

Preparation

Using a green marker, print the words of a Bible memory verse and its reference on large index cards, two or three words on each card. Using a red marker, print definitions of several key words in the verse on the backs of the corresponding cards. Cut cards into puzzle pieces and hide pieces around the room.

Procedure

1. Invite students to find puzzle pieces hidden in the room. Referring to green letters, students put pieces together. Students then tape pieces in place and put cards in verse order, referring to verse in their Bibles as needed.

2. Volunteers take turns reading definitions of words written on the backs of cards.

Rearranged Verse

Materials

❏ Bibles

❏ small sheets of construction paper or large index cards

❏ marker

Preparation

Print the words of a Bible memory verse and its reference on construction paper or index cards, one or two words on each paper or card.

Procedure

Divide class into two groups. One group stands in front of the class holding verse papers or cards you prepared in a mixed-up order. Second group finds verse in their Bibles and takes turns giving instructions for first group to rearrange themselves in verse order ("Nathan, take two steps to your right"). If there are more papers or cards than students, arrange words of one phrase at a time. Students read completed verse aloud together.

BIBLE MEMORY

Rolling Words

Materials

- ❏ Bibles
- ❏ marker
- ❏ roll of light-colored crepe paper
- ❏ tape

Preparation

Unroll crepe paper several feet. On unrolled crepe paper, print words of a Bible memory verse and its reference in mixed-up order and spaced approximately 12 inches (30 cm) apart. Roll up crepe paper again.

Procedure

1. Students sit in a circle (or around a table). Give crepe paper roll to a student who unrolls it until a word is visible. Student tears the paper just past the word and hands the roll to another student, keeping the section with the word written on it. Continue process until all words have been torn off the roll.

2. Students tape words in order, reading verse in Bibles to check their work.

BIBLE MEMORY

Secret Pass

Materials

- ❏ Bibles
- ❏ small index card
- ❏ marker
- ❏ children's music cassette/CD and player

Preparation

Print the words of a Bible memory verse and its reference on a small index card. Think of a question which can be answered by the information given in the verse.

Procedure

1. Students stand in a circle (shoulder-to-shoulder if possible) to play a game similar to Button, Button, Who's Got the Button? Choose one student to be "It." "It" stands in the middle of the circle and closes eyes. Give the verse card to a student in the circle. (Optional: If you have a large group of students, make more than one verse card for students to pass.) "It" opens eyes.

2. As you play music, students pass card around the circle behind their backs, trying to keep "It" from seeing who has the card. When you stop the music, "It" tries to identify who has the card by asking a student the question you prepared. If the student does not have the card, he or she answers "Keep searching," and "It" asks another student. If the student does have the card, he or she answers by reading the verse from a Bible. Student with the card becomes "It." Continue game as time permits.

84

Simon Says Verse

Materials

❏ Bibles

❏ large sheet of paper

❏ marker

Preparation

Print the words of a Bible memory verse on large sheet of paper.

Procedure

1. **We're going to play a game like Simon Says except our game will use words instead of actions. I'll say one word at a time from (verse reference). If it is the correct word, repeat it after me; but if it is not the correct word, don't say anything.** Students find and read the Bible memory verse in their Bibles.

2. Begin play, saying several correct words one at a time before saying an incorrect word. If students repeat incorrect words after you, begin the verse again. Continue process until you successfully complete the verse together. If time permits, invite volunteers to take turns leading the game.

BIBLE MEMORY

Sticky Verses

Materials

❑ Bibles

❑ craft sticks

❑ markers

Preparation

Print the words of a Bible memory verse and its reference on craft sticks, two or three words on each stick (see sketch). Make several sets of sticks, one for each group of three or four students.

Procedure

1. Divide class into three groups. Groups gather in a circle. Mix and distribute all the sticks so that each group has an equal amount.

2. Students find and read verse in their Bibles. Groups arrange sticks in verse order. The first group decides on a stick it doesn't need (a duplicate if possible) and then passes the stick to the group on its right. The second group passes a stick it doesn't need to the right. Play continues until a group has the entire verse in order. Read verse aloud.

" FOR GOD

SO LOVED

THE WORLD

THAT HE GAVE

BIBLE MEMORY

Tape Time

Materials

❑ Bibles

❑ masking tape

❑ marker

Preparation

Print the words of a Bible memory verse and its reference on masking tape with enough space between the words so that the words can be individually torn off. (If you have a smaller number of students than words in the verse, print phrases instead of words.) Tear off the individual words and lightly place the separate pieces of tape on the underside of chairs or tables or on the walls around your classroom. In the same manner, print a paraphrase of the verse on masking tape, but do not distribute pieces.

Procedure

1. Students find the words you've hidden around the classroom. After all words have been found, students find the verse in their Bibles and put the pieces in order, taping them to table or floor. While students complete this task, put the paraphrase pieces around the classroom.

2. **Now find some tape pieces which say this verse in a way which helps us understand it better.** Students find paraphrase pieces, put in order and compare to verse. Students read both the verse and its paraphrase aloud.

BIBLE MEMORY

Tower to Remember

Materials

❑ Bibles

❑ Styrofoam cups

❑ markers

Procedure

1. Divide class into five groups. Assign each group one phrase of a Bible memory verse.

2. Give each group several cups. Students letter words of their phrases on the cups, one word on each cup as shown in sketch. Tell students the reference of the verse. Students read verse in their Bibles and attempt to stack cups in order, end-to-end (see sketch). (Challenge: Students stack all cups together in verse order.)

Verse Circles

Materials

- ❏ Bibles
- ❏ index cards
- ❏ marker
- ❏ carpet square or sheet of construction paper
- ❏ children's music cassette/CD and player

Preparation

Print each word of a Bible memory verse and its reference on a separate index card.

Procedure

1. Students form a circle. Place carpet square or sheet of paper between two students so that it forms a part of the circle. Distribute index cards in a mixed-up order.

2. As you play music, students walk around the circle, stepping on the carpet square as they come to it. When you stop the music, student standing on or near the carpet square places his or her card on floor in the middle of the circle. Students holding words before and after the one on the floor put their cards in the correct places.

3. Continue until all cards have been correctly arranged (students may refer to Bibles for help). Read completed verse in order.

BIBLE MEMORY

Verse Walk

Materials

- ❏ Bible
- ❏ large sheets of paper
- ❏ marker
- ❏ Post-it Notes
- ❏ tape
- ❏ children's music cassette/CD and player

Preparation

Print the words of a Bible memory verse on large sheets of paper, two or three words on each sheet of paper. Place a Post-it Note on each paper near the words. Number phrases in verse order, writing numbers on the Post-it Notes. Tape papers randomly to classroom walls.

Procedure

1. As you play music, students walk around the room. When music stops, each student places his or her hand on the nearest paper. More than one student may touch each paper.

2. Students touching paper with first phrase read phrase aloud. Then group touching the second phrase reads second phrase. Continue until entire verse has been read in the correct order.

3. Repeat activity. After several rounds, remove Post-it Notes to see if students can remember the order of the words.

Word Scramble

Materials

❏ Bibles

❏ large index cards

❏ markers

Preparation

Print each word of a Bible memory verse on a separate large index card, scrambling the letters of each word. (If you have fewer students than words, print more than one word on each card. If you have more students than words, make an additional set and do the activity in two groups.)

Procedure

1. Give each student one or two of the word cards. **Unscramble this word and write it on the other side of the card. Read (verse reference) in your Bible if you need help. Then work with the rest of the students to put the verse in order.**

2. After students have completed verse, read verse aloud together.

BIBLE MEMORY

Writing Relay

Materials

☐ Bibles

☐ large sheets of paper

☐ markers

☐ optional—two stopwatches

Preparation

Print the reference for a Bible memory verse at the top of a large sheet of paper—one paper for each group of up to six students. Place papers on one side of the room. Place a marker and a Bible open to the verse next to each paper.

Procedure

1. Divide class into teams of up to six students. Students line up on the side of the room opposite from papers. At your signal, first student in each line runs to nearest paper, reads the verse and writes first word of the verse on the paper. Student leaves Bible open and returns to tag the next person in line. Second student then runs to find and write second word of the verse. Play continues until one team completes the entire verse. (Optional: Groups use stopwatches to time themselves racing to complete the verse.)

2. When all teams have completed the relay, read the verse aloud together.

KING QUIZ

Read the Bible verses to find the missing letters in the names of some of the most famous Bible kings. Then find the names of all these kings in the word search.

These men were kings between 930 BC and 415 BC.

Ah__ __ (1 Kings 16:33)
Ahaz
Amaziah
Asa
Baasha
__a__id (2 Samuel 2:4)
He__ek__ __h (2 Kings 18:16)
Hoshea
Jehoahaz
Jehoash
Jehoiakim
Jehoram
Jehoshaphat

J__ __u (2 Kings 9:5, 6)
__er__b__am (1 Kings 12:20)
Jo__i__h (2 Kings 23:23)
Jotham
M__na__ __eh (2 Kings 21:1)
Menahem
Omri
Pekah
__eh__b__am (1 Kings 11:43)
S__u __ (1 Samuel 11:15)
S__lo__o__ (1 Kings 1:39)
Uzziah
Zedekiah

```
            B
          C A T
I J Y   O I A M U      P K T
  T E S C   B R S B D   S R D G
S M   K H O F N K M H A S P T L Z O     K I
D L R G A O L J E H O A H A Z G O P R Q V J T
B J P J Z I O E H Q L U A S N D E X L D A E U
D S O E B A M H E M P S L A H A Z C B R M R W
F V N H U K O O M A E H S O H V R F Q E A O Y
H I R U A I N R I N K D J O S I A H A H Z B C
J B T B H M R A A A Y O O P D V W R O I O E
L H L B A T P M H S H B A R T I X L I B A A G
N Y D A I K B U N S V L S Y W H O Z K O H M I
P L V B Z T E C F E J E H O S H A P H A T S K
R N H E Z E K I A H N M E N A H E M U M O I M
T C P L U J E H O A S H H A I K E D E Z Q G O
```

BIBLE CHARACTERS—KINGS

KING QUIZ

Read the Bible verses to find the missing letters in the names of some of the most famous Bible kings. Then find the names of all these kings in the word search.

These men were kings between 930 BC and 415 BC.

Ah **a** **b** (1 Kings 16:33)

Ahaz

Amaziah

Asa

Baasha

D**a** **v** id (2 Samuel 2:4)

He **z** ek **i** **a** h (2 Kings 18:16)

Hoshea

Jehoahaz

Jehoash

Jehoiakim

Jehoram

Jehoshaphat

J **e** **h** u (2 Kings 9:5,6)

J er **o** b **o** am (1 Kings 12:20)

Jo s **i** **a** h (2 Kings 23:23)

Jotham

M **a** na **s** **s** eh (2 Kings 21:1)

Menahem

Omri

Pekah

R eh **o** b **o** am (1 Kings 11:43)

S **a** u **l** (1 Samuel 11:15)

S **o** lo **m** o **n** (1 Kings 1:39)

Uzziah

Zedekiah

Name That Maze

Draw a line to show the correct path through this maze.
The letters along the correct path form the names of
women we read about in the Bible.

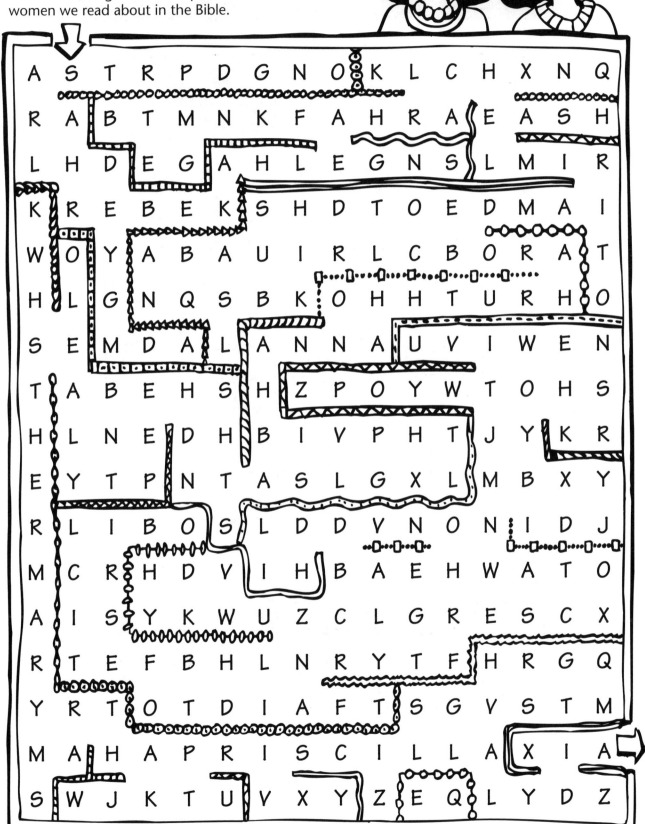

BIBLE CHARACTERS—WOMEN

Name That Maze

Draw a line to show the correct path through this maze. The letters along the correct path form the names of women we read about in the Bible.

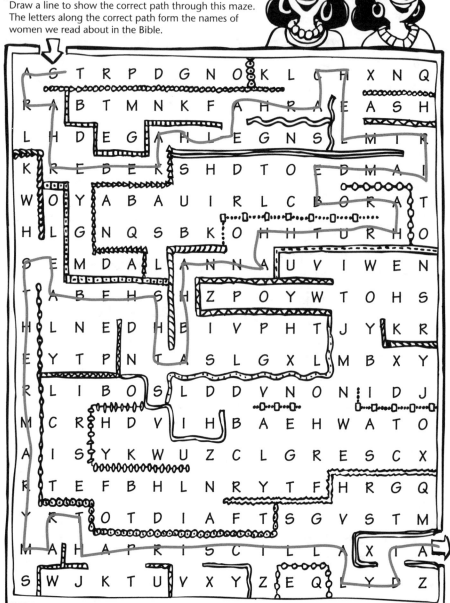

Puzzling Words

Read the Bible verses and fill in the names of these famous people from the book of Acts.

ACROSS

1. He preached about Jesus to a large crowd in Jerusalem. (Acts 2:14)
2. She lived in Philippi and became a Christian after listening to Paul tell about Jesus. (Acts 16:14)
5. The Bible describes this man as so full of God's power that he was able to do many miracles. Later, he was killed because of his faith in God. (Acts 6:8)

DOWN

1. After he believed that Jesus is God's Son, this man traveled to many places telling about Jesus. (Acts 17:2,3)
3. She was known for helping poor widows. (Acts 9:36)
4. This man wrote five books of the New Testament. Four of these books are named after him.
6. He explained the Scriptures to an Ethiopian (Acts 8:26,27,35)

BIBLE CHARACTERS—NEW TESTAMENT

Puzzling Words

Read the Bible verses and fill in the names of these famous people from the book of Acts.

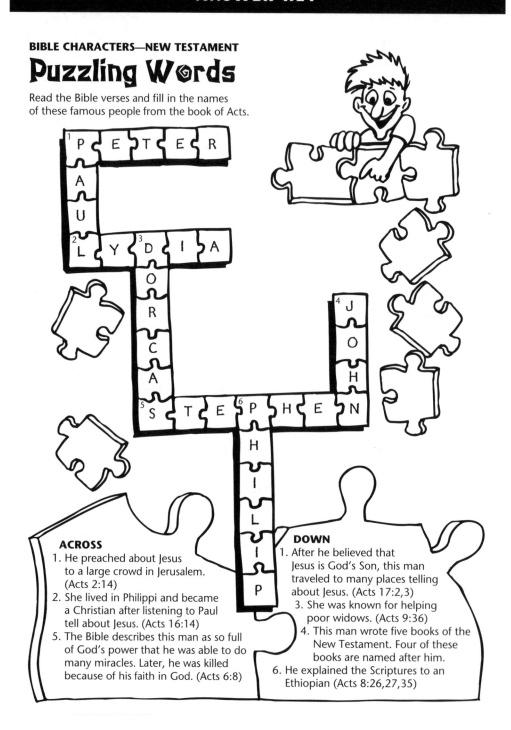

ACROSS

1. He preached about Jesus to a large crowd in Jerusalem. (Acts 2:14)
2. She lived in Philippi and became a Christian after listening to Paul tell about Jesus. (Acts 16:14)
5. The Bible describes this man as so full of God's power that he was able to do many miracles. Later, he was killed because of his faith in God. (Acts 6:8)

DOWN

1. After he believed that Jesus is God's Son, this man traveled to many places telling about Jesus. (Acts 17:2,3)
3. She was known for helping poor widows. (Acts 9:36)
4. This man wrote five books of the New Testament. Four of these books are named after him.
6. He explained the Scriptures to an Ethiopian (Acts 8:26,27,35)

Scrambled Sea Scene

Find the scrambled words hidden in the picture.
Then unscramble them and write them on the lines to name the twelve disciples.

Read Matthew 10:2 to check your answers!

_____ _____

_____ _____

_____ _____

_____ _____

BIBLE CHARACTERS—DISCIPLES

Scrambled Sea Scene

Find the scrambled words hidden in the picture.
Then unscramble them and write them on the lines to name the twelve disciples.

Read Matthew 10:2 to check your answers!

John	Judas
Thomas	Philip
Andrew	Simon
Peter	Matthew
James	James
Bartholomew	Thaddaeus

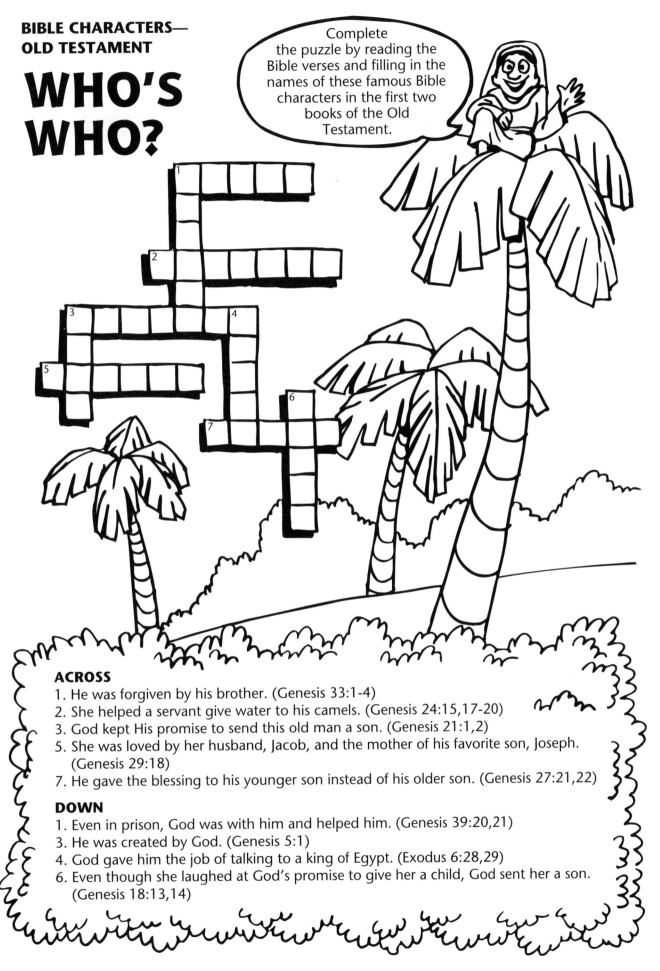

BIBLE CHARACTERS— OLD TESTAMENT

WHO'S WHO?

Complete the puzzle by reading the Bible verses and filling in the names of these famous Bible characters in the first two books of the Old Testament.

ACROSS
1. He was forgiven by his brother. (Genesis 33:1-4)
2. She helped a servant give water to his camels. (Genesis 24:15,17-20)
3. God kept His promise to send this old man a son. (Genesis 21:1,2)
5. She was loved by her husband, Jacob, and the mother of his favorite son, Joseph. (Genesis 29:18)
7. He gave the blessing to his younger son instead of his older son. (Genesis 27:21,22)

DOWN
1. Even in prison, God was with him and helped him. (Genesis 39:20,21)
3. He was created by God. (Genesis 5:1)
4. God gave him the job of talking to a king of Egypt. (Exodus 6:28,29)
6. Even though she laughed at God's promise to give her a child, God sent her a son. (Genesis 18:13,14)

**BIBLE CHARACTERS—
OLD TESTAMENT**

WHO'S WHO?

Complete the puzzle by reading the Bible verses and filling in the names of these famous Bible characters in the first two books of the Old Testament.

ACROSS
1. He was forgiven by his brother. (Genesis 33:1-4)
2. She helped a servant give water to his camels. (Genesis 24:15,17-20)
3. God kept His promise to send this old man a son. (Genesis 21:1,2)
5. She was loved by her husband, Jacob, and the mother of his favorite son, Joseph. (Genesis 29:18)
7. He gave the blessing to his younger son instead of his older son. (Genesis 27:21,22)

DOWN
1. Even in prison, God was with him and helped him. (Genesis 39:20,21)
3. He was created by God. (Genesis 5:1)
4. God gave him the job of talking to a king of Egypt. (Exodus 6:28,29)
6. Even though she laughed at God's promise to give her a child, God sent her a son. (Genesis 18:13,14)

AMAZING WAYS

Find your way through the maze to match each word with its definition.
If you need help, look up the word in a Bible dictionary.

FAITH

HOLY

GRACE

MIRACLE

To be perfect and without sin; belonging to God.

An event or wonderful happening done by the power of God.

To be certain about the things we cannot see.

Love and kindness shown to a person who does not deserve it.

BIBLE DICTIONARY

AMAZING WAYS

Find your way through the maze to match each word with its definition.
If you need help, look up the word in a Bible dictionary.

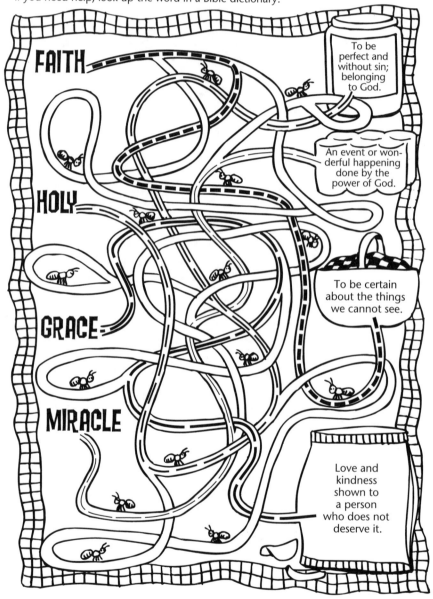

Dot Definitions

Connect the dots to find four words (each "1" begins a new letter). Use a Bible dictionary to find the definition of each word, and then draw lines to match each word with its definition. (Watch out for the extra definition!)

An agreement between God and His people.

To buy back. Jesus paid the price to "buy us back" and set us free from our slavery to sin.

To make someone angry on purpose.

To make up for a wrong act. Jesus did this by dying on the cross for our sins.

Using water to show that someone is a member of God's family.

BIBLE DICTIONARY

Dot Definitions

Connect the dots to find four words (each "1" begins a new letter). Use a Bible dictionary to find the definition of each word, and then draw lines to match each word with its definition. (Watch out for the extra definition!)

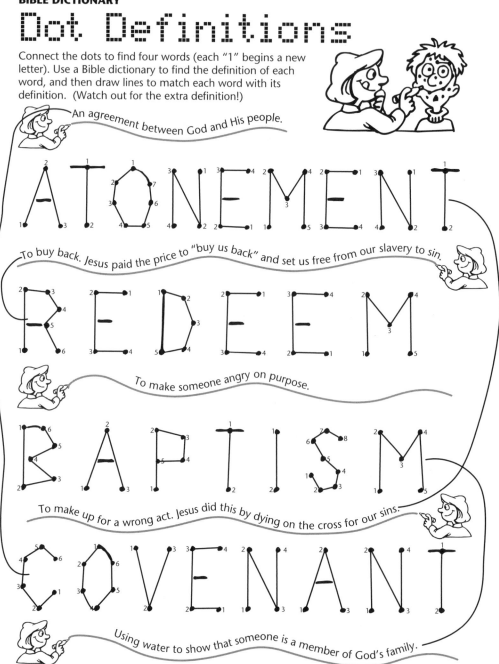

An agreement between God and His people.

ATONEMENT

To buy back. Jesus paid the price to "buy us back" and set us free from our slavery to sin.

REDEEM

To make someone angry on purpose.

BAPTISM

To make up for a wrong act. Jesus did this by dying on the cross for our sins.

COVENANT

Using water to show that someone is a member of God's family.

BIBLE DICTIONARY

WORD ☐
WORKS

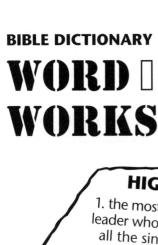

Use a Bible dictionary to help you circle the correct definition for each of the words below.

PASSOVER:

7. a name for Jesus.

8. one of the Jews' most important feasts; celebrated as a reminder that God freed them from slavery in Egypt.

9. a special food God gave the Israelites in the desert.

HIGH PRIEST:

1. the most important Temple leader who made sacrifices for all the sins of the Hebrews.

2. one of the prophets who told God's message to the Israelites.

3. a person who settled arguments between two people.

TITHE:

10. a small harp.

11. to give God one-tenth of what you have.

12. to go against the rights of someone else.

GENTILE:

4. a short story that teaches a lesson.

5. everlasting; having no beginning or end.

6. any person who is not a Jew.

TABERNACLE:

13. a Hebrew word that means "church."

14. the portable tent where the Israelites worshiped God.

15. the place where grain was trampled by oxen.

Now color in the squares containing the numbers you circled above. When all the squares are correctly colored in, you will find the word that means to tell God or others about your sins.

1	1	1	2	1	1	1	2	1	2	3	2	1	3	1	1	1	3	1	1	1	2	1	1	1	2	1	1
6	5	5	4	6	4	6	4	6	6	5	5	6	4	6	4	4	5	6	4	4	5	6	4	5	4	6	4
8	7	9	7	8	9	8	7	8	9	8	7	8	9	8	8	8	7	8	8	8	9	8	8	8	7	8	8
11	12	10	12	11	10	11	10	11	12	12	11	11	10	11	12	10	12	11	12	10	10	10	12	11	10	12	10
14	14	14	15	14	14	14	15	14	13	13	13	14	15	14	13	13	15	14	14	14	14	13	14	14	15	14	14

BIBLE DICTIONARY

WORD ☐
WORKS

Use a Bible dictionary to help you circle the correct definition for each of the words below.

PASSOVER:

7. a name for Jesus.

(8. one of the Jews' most important feasts; celebrated as a reminder that God freed them from slavery in Egypt.)

9. a special food God gave the Israelites in the desert.

HIGH PRIEST:

(1. the most important Temple leader who made sacrifices for all the sins of the Hebrews.)

2. one of the prophets who told God's message to the Israelites.

3. a person who settled arguments between two people.

TITHE:

10. a small harp.

(11. to give God one-tenth of what you have.)

12. to go against the rights of someone else.

GENTILE:

4. a short story that teaches a lesson.

5. everlasting; having no beginning or end.

(6. any person who is not a Jew.)

TABERNACLE:

13. a Hebrew word that means "church."

(14. the portable tent where the Israelites worshiped God.)

15. the place where grain was trampled by oxen.

Now color in the squares containing the numbers you circled above. When all the squares are correctly colored in, you will find the word that means to tell God or others about your sins.

1	1	1	2	1	1	1	2	1	2	3	2	1	3	1	1	1	3	1	1	1	2	1	1	1	2	1	1	1
6	5	5	4	6	4	6	4	6	6	5	5	6	4	6	4	4	5	6	4	5	6	4	5	4	6	4	4
8	7	9	7	8	9	8	7	8	9	8	7	8	9	8	8	8	7	8	8	8	9	8	8	8	7	8	8	8
11	12	10	12	11	10	11	10	11	12	12	11	11	10	11	12	10	12	11	12	10	10	10	12	11	10	12	10	11
14	14	14	15	14	14	14	15	14	13	13	13	14	15	14	13	13	15	14	14	14	13	14	14	14	15	14	14	14

Code Fill In

A = __ books in the Old Testament
D = __ books in the Gospels
E = __ followers sent by Jesus
to tell about Him
(Luke 9:1, 2)
H = __ gifts of the wise men
(Matthew 2:11)
J = __ books in the New
Testament
M = __ books in the Bible
P = __ chapters in Genesis
R = __ chapters in Acts
S = __ chapters in Revelation
U = __ verses in the Bible's longest chapter
(Psalm 119)
V = __ days it rained while Noah was in the ark (Genesis 7:12)
W = __ years Joseph lived (Genesis 50:22)

Use your Bible to fill in the missing numbers. Then use the code to discover two very important words.

___ ___ O ___ T L ___ = ___ ___ ___ ___ ___ O N
39 50   22   12   39   50 12 28 22

___ ___ N T ___ O ___ T ___ ___ ___ ___ ___
22 12   176   39 22   39

___ ___ ___ ___ ___ N G ___ ___ .
66 12 22 22 12   12 28

___ I T N ___ ___ ___ = T O ___ T ___ L L
110   12 22 22   12

O T ___ ___ ___ ___ ___ ___ ___ T ___ Y O ___
3 12 28 22   110 3 39   176

___ ___ ___ ___ ___ ___ ___ N .
3 39 40 12   22 12 12

T ___ ___ ___ ___ O ___ T L ___ ___
3 12   39 50   22   12 22

___ I T N ___ ___ ___ ___ ___ ___ B O ___ T
110   12 22 22 12 4   39   176

___ ___ ___ ___ ___ .
27 12 22 176 22

BIBLE WORD DEFINITIONS

Code Fill In

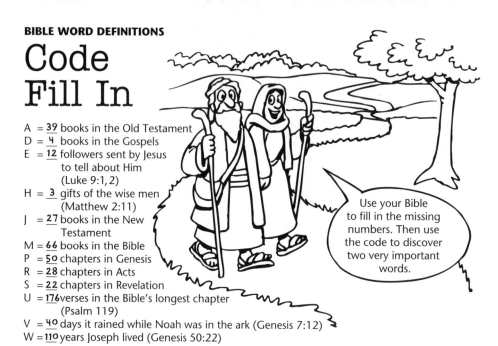

A = **39** books in the Old Testament
D = **4** books in the Gospels
E = **12** followers sent by Jesus
    to tell about Him
    (Luke 9:1, 2)
H = **3** gifts of the wise men
    (Matthew 2:11)
J = **27** books in the New
    Testament
M = **66** books in the Bible
P = **50** chapters in Genesis
R = **28** chapters in Acts
S = **22** chapters in Revelation
U = **176** verses in the Bible's longest chapter
    (Psalm 119)
V = **40** days it rained while Noah was in the ark (Genesis 7:12)
W = **110** years Joseph lived (Genesis 50:22)

Use your Bible to fill in the missing numbers. Then use the code to discover two very important words.

A P O S T L E = A P E R S O N
39 50 22   12 39 50 12 28 22

S E N T   O U T   A S   A
22 12   176   39 22   39

M E S S E N G E R.
66 12 22 22 12   12 28

W I T N E S S = T O   T E L L
110   12 22 22   12

O T H E R S   W H A T   Y O U
  3 12 28 22   110 3 39   176

H A V E   S E E N.
3 39 40 12   22 12 12

T H E   A P O S T L E S
  3 12   39 50   22   12 22

W I T N E S S E D   A B O U T
110   12 22 22 12 4   39   176

J E S U S.
27 12 22 176 22

DOMINO DEFINITION

COLOR ☐ IN THE ☐ SQUARES:

ORANGE

YELLOW

BLUE

A PLACE IN BIBLE TIMES WHERE A GIFT OR OFFERING (SACRIFICE) ☐ WAS GIVEN TO GOD TO WORSHIP HIM; MADE OF DIRT, STONES OR WOOD.

BIBLE WORD DEFINITIONS

DOMINO DEFINITION

COLOR IN THE SQUARES:

ORANGE

YELLOW

BLUE

A PLACE IN BIBLE TIMES WHERE A GIFT OR OFFERING (SACRIFICE) WAS GIVEN TO GOD TO WORSHIP HIM; MADE OF DIRT, STONES OR WOOD.

Ferris Wheel Definitions

Letters on the wheel (clockwise from arrow): H G E O C D Y P R R E O V P E H L E A T T C I H O O N S M E A N K B E Y K G N O O D W W N R H I T D E S P E N E U A N K K P N R O O W P N

___ ___ ___ ___ ___ ___ ___ : a man or woman

___ ___ ___ ___ ___ ___   ___ ___ ___ ___ ___

to ___ ___ ___ ___ ___   or ___ ___ ___ ___ ___ God's

message (___ ___ ___ ___ ___ ___ ___ ___) to others.

___ ___ ___ ___ ___ ___ ___ ___ ___ ___ ___ : to

___ ___ ___ ___   ___ ___ ___ ___ ___ ___ something that was

___ ___ ___ ___ ___ ___   or ___ ___ ___ ___ ___ ___ ___ .

(___ ___ ___ shows what He is like

through His actions and the

world He made.)

Begin at the arrow and write every other letter in order on the blank lines. Cross off the letters on the Ferris wheel as you move around it. Keep going until the puzzle is complete. You will find the definitions of two words that help us understand more about God's messages.

Bonus: Read Jonah 3:8,9 to find out what one prophet said.

BIBLE WORD DEFINITIONS

Ferris Wheel Definitions

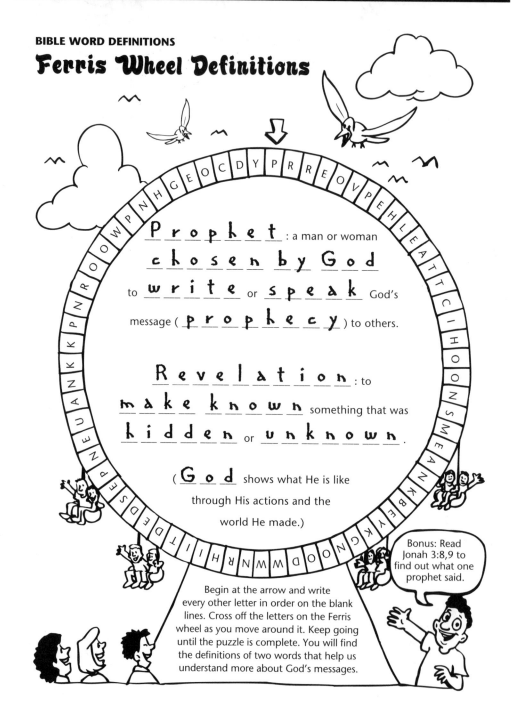

Prophet : a man or woman **chosen by God** to **write** or **speak** God's message (**prophecy**) to others.

Revelation : to **make known** something that was **hidden** or **unknown**.

(**God** shows what He is like through His actions and the world He made.)

Begin at the arrow and write every other letter in order on the blank lines. Cross off the letters on the Ferris wheel as you move around it. Keep going until the puzzle is complete. You will find the definitions of two words that help us understand more about God's messages.

Bonus: Read Jonah 3:8,9 to find out what one prophet said.

BIBLE WORD DEFINITIONS

True or False?

Circle the letter under the **T** if the sentence is true. Circle the letter under the **F** if the sentence if false. You will need to use your Bible to find some of the answers.

1. There are 27 Gospels.
2. There are 39 Old Testament books.
3. The book of Romans was written by Paul (see Romans 1:1).
4. The book of Titus was written by Titus (see Titus 1:1,4).
5. Acts tells what the followers of Jesus did to teach others about Him.
6. There are 150 Psalms (poems or songs which praise God).
7. The book of Amos comes after the book of Jonah.
8. There are three sets of books which have the same name in the Old Testament and five sets in the New Testament.
9. Leviticus 19:11 could help you decide whether or not to tell the truth.
10. Philemon comes after Titus.
11. Ezekiel comes before Daniel.
12. 1 John 4:9 tells about God's love for us.
13. Genesis is the first book of the New Testament.
14. The book of Jonah is in the New Testament.
15. Matthew, Mark, Luke and John all tell the stories of Jesus' life.
16. Malachi is the last book of the Old Testament.
17. 1 Corinthians has more chapters than 2 Corinthians.
18. The book which talks about someone being thrown in a lions' den is called Daniel.
19. The book of Exodus talks about the Israelites exiting, or leaving, Egypt.
20. The book of Revelation is in the Old Testament.
21. There are four books in the New Testament which have the word "John" in their name.

	T	F
1.	S	S
2.	C	C
3.	R	R
4.	I	I
5.	P	B
6.	T	E
7.	S	U
8.	R	C
9.	E	O
10.	M	P
11.	E	I
12.	A	E
13.	D	N
14.	G	S
15.	W	O
16.	R	D
17.	I	S
18.	T	L
19.	I	A
20.	W	N
21.	G	S

Write the circled letters in order in the numbered boxes to find an important definition.

(Another name for the Bible is "Holy Scripture.")

Write the uncircled letters in order in these numbered boxes to find out who copied the Scriptures onto scrolls.

1 2 3 4 5 6 7 8 9 10 11 12 13 14 15 16 17 18 19 20 21

1 2 3 4 5 6 7 8 9 10 11 12 13 14 15 16 17 18 19 20 21

BIBLE WORD DEFINITIONS

True or False?

Circle the letter under the **T** if the sentence is true. Circle the letter under the **F** if the sentence if false. You will need to use your Bible to find some of the answers.

1. There are 27 Gospels.
2. There are 39 Old Testament books.
3. The book of Romans was written by Paul (see Romans 1:1).
4. The book of Titus was written by Titus (see Titus 1:1,4).
5. Acts tells what the followers of Jesus did to teach others about Him.
6. There are 150 Psalms (poems or songs which praise God).
7. The book of Amos comes after the book of Jonah.
8. There are three sets of books which have the same name in the Old Testament and five sets in the New Testament.
9. Leviticus 19:11 could help you decide whether or not to tell the truth.
10. Philemon comes after Titus.
11. Ezekiel comes before Daniel.
12. 1 John 4:9 tells about God's love for us.
13. Genesis is the first book of the New Testament.
14. The book of Jonah is in the New Testament.
15. Matthew, Mark, Luke and John all tell the stories of Jesus' life.
16. Malachi is the last book of the Old Testament.
17. 1 Corinthians has more chapters than 2 Corinthians.
18. The book which talks about someone being thrown in a lions' den is called Daniel.
19. The book of Exodus talks about the Israelites exiting, or leaving, Egypt.
20. The book of Revelation is in the Old Testament.
21. There are four books in the New Testament which have the word "John" in their name.

	T	F
1.	S	(S)
2.	(C)	C
3.	(R)	R
4.	I	(I)
5.	(P)	B
6.	(T)	E
7.	S	(U)
8.	(R)	C
9.	(E)	O
10.	(M)	P
11.	(E)	I
12.	(A)	E
13.	D	(N)
14.	G	(S)
15.	(W)	O
16.	(R)	D
17.	(I)	S
18.	(T)	L
19.	(I)	A
20.	W	(N)
21.	(G)	S

(Another name for the Bible is "Holy Scripture.")

Write the circled letters in order in the numbered boxes to find an important definition.

Write the uncircled letters in order in these numbered boxes to find out who copied the Scriptures onto scrolls.

SCRIPTURE MEANS WRITING

SCRIBES COPIED GOD'S LAWS

BIBLE BOOKS
Bible Book Basics

Draw an arrow in the box to show which way you have to go in your Bible to move from the first book listed to the second book listed.

FROM   TO

Psalms [ ] Leviticus

Mark [ ] John

1 Corinthians [ ] Ephesians

Romans [ ] 1 Thessalonians

Jeremiah [ ] Micah

Haggai [ ] 1 Kings

Ezekiel [ ] Acts

Use your Bible to fill in the correct answers.

The book

before Ecclesiastes _____

after Joshua _____

before Jude _____

after Ezra _____

before Micah _____

after Luke _____

before 1 Peter _____

after Job _____

Fill in the answers to the Cross puzzles.

Down—Paul's letter to the church in Ephesus.
Across—First book of the Bible.

Down—Fifth book in the Old Testament.
Across—New Testament book starting with *H*.

Down—First book of the New Testament.
Across—Last of Paul's letters beginning with the letter *T*.

Down—Either one of two of the books of Prophecy would fit here.
Across—Book of Prophecy beginning with *N*.

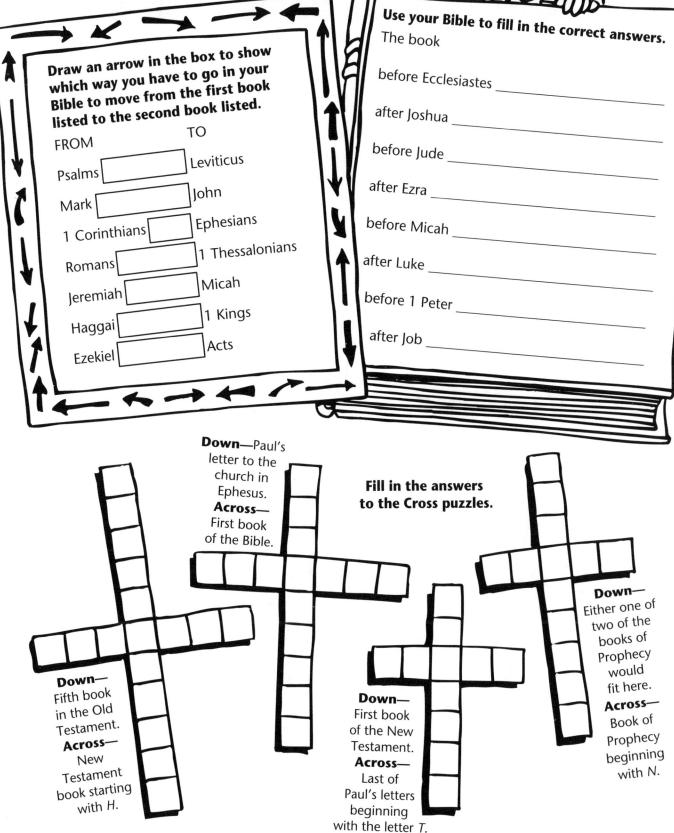

BIBLE BOOKS

Bible Book Basics

Draw an arrow in the box to show which way you have to go in your Bible to move from the first book listed to the second book listed.

FROM   TO

Psalms   ←   Leviticus

Mark   →   John

1 Corinthians   →   Ephesians

Romans   →   1 Thessalonians

Jeremiah   →   Micah

Haggai   ←   1 Kings

Ezekiel   →   Acts

Use your Bible to fill in the correct answers.

The book

before Ecclesiastes   *Proverbs*

after Joshua   *Judges*

before Jude   *3 John*

after Ezra   *Nehemiah*

before Micah   *Jonah*

after Luke   *John*

before 1 Peter   *James*

after Job   *Psalms*

Fill in the answers to the Cross puzzles.

Down—Paul's letter to the church in Ephesus.
Across—First book of the Bible.

Down—Fifth book in the Old Testament.
Across—New Testament book starting with H.

DEUTERONOMY

HEBREWS

EPHESIANS

GENESIS

Down—First book of the New Testament.
Across—Last of Paul's letters beginning with the letter T.

MATTHEW

TITUS

ZECHARIAH

NAHUM

Down—Either one of two of the books of Prophecy would fit here.
Zephaniah or Zechariah
Across—Book of Prophecy beginning with N.

BIBLE BOOKS

Follow the Clues

1. It is not in any of the books which are laying flat.
2. It is to the left of Romans.
3. It is not a book which has the same name as another book.
4. It has more than four letters in its name.
5. It has the same name as something in an address.

One of the books below has a story about a talking animal. Find where the story is by reading the clues below.

Read _____ 22:21-34 for the story about what happened!
(book you discovered)

In one of the books below you can read about two miraculous escapes from prison.

1. It is not any of the books which are stacked in a pile.
2. It is to the right of Exodus.
3. It is not a book with a person's name.
4. It is not an Old Testament book.

Read _____ 12:5-11 and 16:16-40 for the story about who escaped from prison!
(book you discovered)

ANSWER KEY

BIBLE BOOKS

Follow the Clues

One of the books below has a story about a talking animal. Find where the story is by reading the clues below.

1. It is not in any of the books which are laying flat.
2. It is to the left of Romans.
3. It is not a book which has the same name as another book.
4. It has more than four letters in its name.
5. It has the same name as something in an address.

Read _____Numbers_____ 22:21-34 for the story about what happened!
(book you discovered)

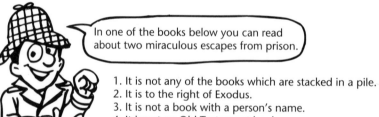

In one of the books below you can read about two miraculous escapes from prison.

1. It is not any of the books which are stacked in a pile.
2. It is to the right of Exodus.
3. It is not a book with a person's name.
4. It is not an Old Testament book.

Read _____Acts_____ 12:5-11 and 16:16-40 for the story about who escaped from prison!
(book you discovered)

Hidden Word

Color each space which contains the name of a book of the Bible. Then turn the paper until you can read what word the colored spaces spell.

Genesis	Hannah	Ishmael	Exodus	Law	Obed	Leviticus
Numbers	Letters	Naomi	Deuteronomy	Caleb	Prophets	Joshua
Judges	Ruth	1 Samuel	2 Samuel	1 Kings	2 Kings	1 Chronicles
Abraham	Ezariah	Narnia	Madagascar	Ethiopia	Song of Simon	1 Queen
2 Queen	3 Queen	Jacob	Zeborias	Judah	Priest	2 Chronicles
Singing	Poetry	Rebekah	Methuselah	Rabbi	Nathan	Ezra
Nehemiah	Esther	Job	Psalms	Proverbs	Ecclesiastes	Song of Songs
Pharisee	1 David	2 David	Mordecai	Isaac	Carl	Rahab
Isaiah	Jeremiah	Lamentations	Ezekiel	Daniel	Hosea	Joel
Amos	Namon	Rachel	Obadiah	Joseph	Danny	Jonah
Micah	Nahum	Habakkuk	Zephaniah	Haggai	Zechariah	Malachi
Deborah	Edom	Abigail	Reuben	Levi	Bartholomew	History
Matthew	Philip	Peter	Thaddeus	Judas	Mary	Mark
Luke	John	Acts	Romans	1 Corinthians	2 Corinthians	Galatians
Ephesians	Rome	Galapagos	Hannibal	Lyonius	Grecians	Philippians
Balaam	Solomon	Leah	Barnabas	Salonichus	1 Torah	2 Torah
Colossians	1 Thessalonians	2 Thessalonians	1 Timothy	2 Timothy	Titus	Philemon
Hebrews	Saloam	Seth	James	Abel	Andrew	1 Peter
2 Peter	1 John	2 John	3 John	Jude	Revelation	

Hint: Look at the contents page of your Bible for help!

BIBLE BOOKS

Hidden Word

Color each space which contains the name of a book of the Bible. Then turn the paper until you can read what word the colored spaces spell.

Genesis	Hannah	Ishmael	Exodus	Law	Obed	Leviticus
Numbers	Letters	Naomi	Deuteronomy	Caleb	Prophets	Joshua
Judges	Ruth	1 Samuel	2 Samuel	1 Kings	2 Kings	1 Chronicles
Abraham	Ezariah	Narnia	Madagascar	Ethiopia	Song of Simon	1 Queen
2 Queen	3 Queen	Jacob	Zeborias	Judah	Priest	2 Chronicles
Singing	Poetry	Rebekah	Methuselah	Rabbi	Nathan	Ezra
Nehemiah	Esther	Job	Psalms	Proverbs	Ecclesiastes	Song of Songs
Pharisee	1 David	2 David	Mordecai	Isaac	Carl	Rahab
Isaiah	Jeremiah	Lamentations	Ezekiel	Daniel	Hosea	Joel
Amos	Namon	Rachel	Obadiah	Joseph	Danny	Jonah
Micah	Nahum	Habakkuk	Zephaniah	Haggai	Zechariah	Malachi
Deborah	Edom	Abigail	Reuben	Levi	Bartholomew	History
Matthew	Philip	Peter	Thaddeus	Judas	Mary	Mark
Luke	John	Acts	Romans	1 Corinthians	2 Corinthians	Galatians
Ephesians	Rome	Galapagos	Hannibal	Lyonius	Grecians	Philippians
Balaam	Solomon	Leah	Barnabas	Salonichus	1 Torah	2 Torah
Colossians	1 Thessalonians	2 Thessalonians	1 Timothy	2 Timothy	Titus	Philemon
Hebrews	Saloam	Seth	James	Abel	Andrew	1 Peter
2 Peter	1 John	2 John	3 John	Jude	Revelation	

Hint: Look at the contents page of your Bible for help!

OLD TESTAMENT SURPRISE

Color in each section that contains a book of the Old Testament. You'll find a picture of someone who is not found anywhere in the Bible.

JOB
LAMENTATIONS
OBADIAH
JOSHUA
ECCLESIASTES
HOSEA
DANIEL
2 KINGS
NAHUM
SONG OF SONGS
2 CHRONICLES
ZEPHANIAH
1 KINGS
EZEKIEL
JONAH
JOB
NAHUM
JOEL
LYNNETTE
KYLE
WILL
EZRA
HAGGAI
BILL
MOSES
PROVERBS
1 CHRONICLES
ZECHARIAH
ERIC
JOHN
NEHEMIAH
AMOS
ISAIAH
KARIN
AMOS
EXODUS
NUMBERS
RYAN
MARY
RUTH
LEVITICUS
LEO
KATIE
HABAKKUK
ANNA
AMY
JUDGES
MICAH
JEREMIAH
HOSEA
RILEY
JOB
JOEL
2 KINGS
HOSEA
AMOS
MALACHI
TIM
FRED
JOSEPHINE
DYLAN
PSALMS
GENESIS
CHRIS
ANDREW
2 SAMUEL
LEVITICUS
EZEKIEL
JOB
NOEL
DEBBIE
FIDO
SUSAN
NUMBERS
HEATHER
EXODUS
ISAIAH
1 SAMUEL
OBADIAH
KATIE
ELI
JONAH
ESTHER
JIM
DANIEL
RUTH
LEVITICUS
AARON
LINDA
AMANDA
SAMANTHA
MALACHI
MALACHI
JOB
EXODUS
DEUTERONOMY
ISAIAH
DANIEL
EZRA
MICAH
HAGGAI
JEN
JOB
1 SAMUEL
PROVERBS
DEUTERONOMY
ECCLESIASTES
AMOS
RUTH
2 KINGS
HOSEA
JEREMIAH

(Hint: Use the contents page in your Bible.)

BIBLE BOOKS—OLD TESTAMENT

OLD TESTAMENT SURPRISE

Color in each section that contains a book of the Old Testament. You'll find a picture of someone who is not found anywhere in the Bible.

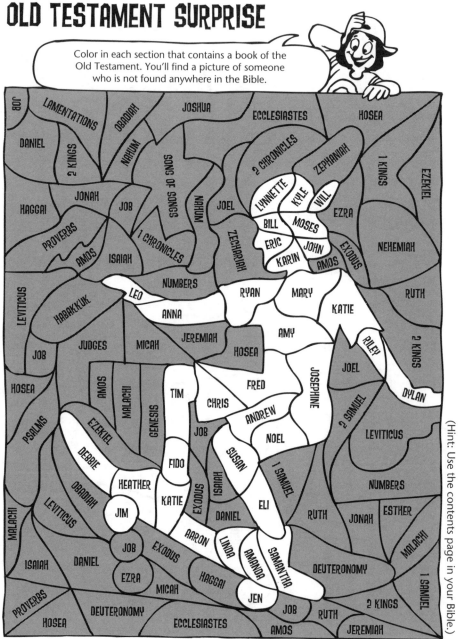

(Hint: Use the contents page in your Bible.)

Bubble Gum

Follow the lines to move between each gum ball, spelling the names of the New Testament books written on each machine. You may move in any direction.

PAUL'S LETTERS

Romans
Corinthians (1,2)
Galatians
Ephesians
Philippians
Colossians
Thessalonians (1,2)
Timothy (1,2)
Titus
Philemon

Matthew
Mark
Luke
John
Acts

GOSPELS & HISTORY

Hebrews
James
Peter (1,2)
John (1,2,3)
Jude
Revelation

GENERAL LETTERS & PROPHECY

BIBLE BOOKS—NEW TESTAMENT

Bubble Gum

Follow the lines to move between each gum ball, spelling the names of the New Testament books written on each machine. You may move in any direction.

Matthew
Mark
Luke
John
Acts

GOSPELS & HISTORY

Romans
Corinthians (1,2)
Galatians
Ephesians
Philippians
Colossians
Thessalonians (1,2)
Timothy (1,2)
Titus
Philemon

PAUL'S LETTERS

Hebrews
James
Peter (1,2)
John (1,2,3)
Jude
Revelation

GENERAL LETTERS & PROPHECY

Computer Art

Start at the arrow and draw a line through all the letters that spell the books of the New Testament in order. You may move in any direction. When you are finished, you will see a picture of an animal people used for travel in Bible times.

V	D	B	L	I	N	T	R	B	G	F	D	H	A	B	Q	P	S	T	L	D	A	E	G	R	V	L	T
J	L	O	E	Q	S	T	O	M	V	B	T	S	R	C	K	R	F	O	R	E	U	L	C	J	K	Y	Q
S	T	U	G	I	F	R	E	O	J	Y	C	E	O	M	D	O	L	U	T	J	D	V	O	R	P	X	Z
D	S	B	F	M	I	V	F	Q	T	N	A	W	R	B	A	E	G	Q	P	K	F	R	C	I	N	T	V
C	W	O	D	T	A	O	P	Z	O	H	A	J	S	E	N	S	1	C	Q	U	H	K	2	X	A	I	H
E	Y	K	L	E	U	K	G	E	J	M	J	3	N	H	N	O	M	O	R	H	D	T	S	S	N	O	F
N	J	G	F	I	B	L	U	K	E	H	O	O	I	H	O	J	E	L	I	N	P	A	N	G	Q	L	U
K	F	M	A	W	R	K	1	S	J	N	X	N	T	A	L	2	N	I	H	T	H	I	L	A	K	E	R
V	A	U	C	M	A	P	X	U	D	E	R	E	V	E	1	J	O	H	P	S	U	T	A	F	O	M	W
R	N	L	K	W	E	T	E	R	2	P	E	T	E	R	T	H	Y	T	I	T	A	I	M	W	B	Q	T
U	F	H	E	A	S	1	T	I	M	O	T	2	I	M	O	L	O	C	S	S	N	Q	K	Q	L	M	R
W	S	T	I	N	N	S	S	E	H	T	H	Y	T	S	S	O	P	N	L	E	B	F	U	O	U	C	H
E	D	T	B	O	M	A	J	D	M	1	S	N	A	I	D	K	G	A	K	P	M	A	B	E	L	E	O
K	A	R	F	L	P	L	E	W	L	V	F	Q	B	J	F	Q	C	I	T	H	K	W	A	J	A	H	T
M	F	O	W	A	T	V	O	Q	E	U	I	D	R	T	K	M	U	P	R	E	O	E	M	N	F	K	N
T	L	R	Q	S	F	H	N	C	D	L	V	A	W	O	Q	F	I	P	O	S	B	Z	Q	R	B	P	U
A	W	L	S	I	M	C	I	F	W	E	B	N	D	R	C	W	L	T	D	I	Q	I	E	N	A	D	E
E	J	F	E	C	R	P	A	D	K	T	P	Q	M	A	E	U	I	R	Q	A	F	K	B	J	S	L	A
M	P	I	H	T	2	S	N	C	S	R	N	O	L	Y	N	O	H	P	S	N	P	A	M	S	O	N	F

HINT: USE THE CONTENTS PAGE OF YOUR BIBLE FOR HELP.

BIBLE BOOKS—NEW TESTAMENT

Computer Art

Start at the arrow and draw a line through all the letters that spell the books of the New Testament in order. You may move in any direction. When you are finished, you will see a picture of an animal people used for travel in Bible times.

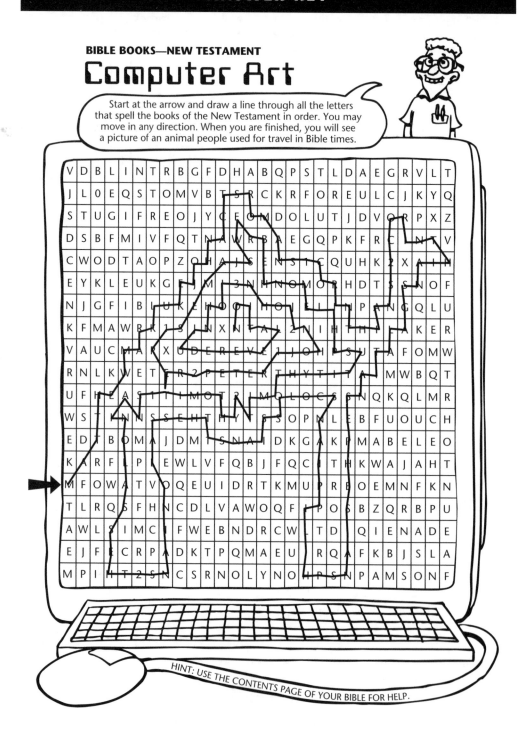

HINT: USE THE CONTENTS PAGE OF YOUR BIBLE FOR HELP.

Swimming Divisions

POOL RULES:
(2) Find the Old Testament book names written below. Draw a line to match each set of books to its division above.

(1) To discover the names of the Old Testament divisions, follow the arrows and change each letter in the inner tubes to the letter that comes before it in the alphabet. Write the name you find on the line below each inner tube.

I S A I A H J E R E M I A H L A M E N T A T I

O N S E Z E K I E L D A N I E L H O S E A J

O E L A M O S O B A D I A H J O N A H M I C

A H N A H U M H A B A K K U K Z E P H A N I

A H H A G G A I Z E C H A R I A H M A L A C H I

Inner tubes (letters):
- N → I → J → T → U → P → S
- M ↓ X ← B
- Z → Q → P → F → U → S
- P → I → F → D → Z → Q → S

Turtle shell: LEVITICUSNUMBERSDEUTERONOMYGENESISEXODUS

J O B P S A L M S P R O V E R B S E C C L E S I A S T E S S O N G O F S O N G S

J O S H U A J U D G E S R U T H F I R S T S
T S R I F L E U M A S D N O C E S L E U M A
K I N G S S E C O N D K I N G S F I R S T C
I N O R H C D N O C E S S E L C I N O R H
C L E S E Z R A N E H E M I A H E S T H E R

BIBLE DIVISIONS—OLD TESTAMENT

Swimming Divisions

POOL RULES:
(2) Find the Old Testament book names written below. Draw a line to match each set of books to its division above.

(1) To discover the names of the Old Testament divisions, follow the arrows and change each letter in the inner tubes to the letter that comes before it in the alphabet. Write the name you find on the line below each inner tube.

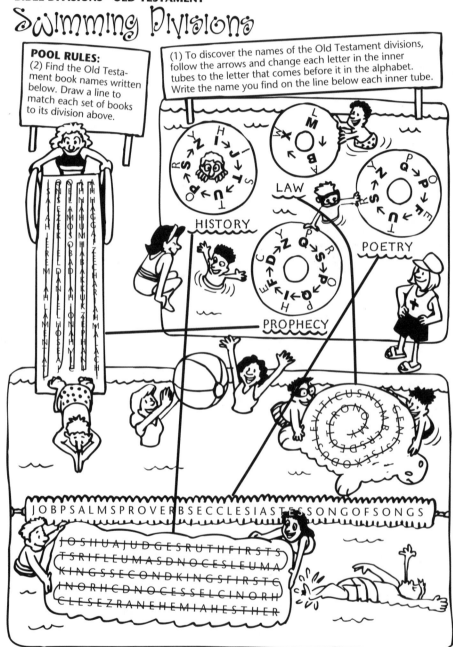

HISTORY

LAW

POETRY

PROPHECY

JOBPSALMSPROVERBSECCLESIASTESSONGOFSONGS

JOSHUAJUDGESRUTHFIRSTS
TSRIFLEUMASDNOCESLEUMA
KINGSSECONDKINGSFIRSTC
INORHCDNOCESSELCINORH
CLESEZRANEHEMIAHESTHER

Turn and Match

Cut out the shapes at the bottom of the page. Place the shapes on the game board, turning them until the same word is matched on all connecting sides. Then read the verses in your Bible to find what God promises.

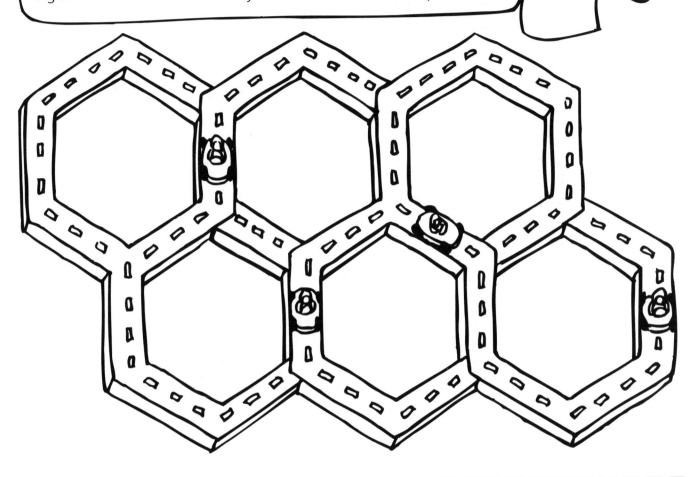

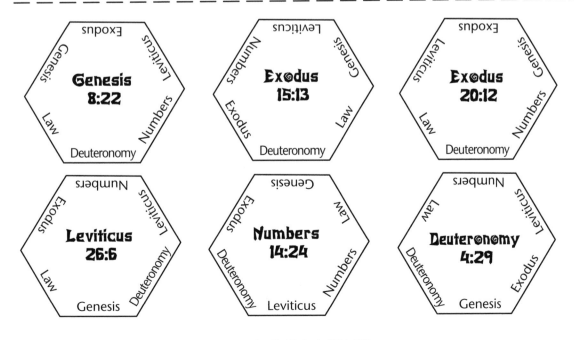

BIBLE DIVISIONS—OLD TESTAMENT LAW

Turn and Match

Cut out the shapes at the bottom of the page. Place the shapes on the game board, turning them until the same word is matched on all connecting sides. Then read the verses in your Bible to find what God promises.

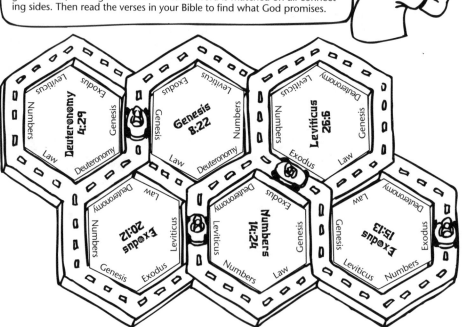

WALKING WITH THE ISRAELITES

Choose a number from 1 to 17. Follow the path and look for the sandals with the number you chose. Write the letters in order on the blank line with the same number. Repeat with other numbers until the blank lines are filled.

START

6·JOS
10·2 SAMU
13·ONICLES
15·EZRA
2·EXOD
13·1 CHR
4·NUM

11·1 KINGS
5·DEUTERO
4·BERS
9·1 S
3·LEV
16·NEH
17·EST
16·EMIAH

5·NOMY
10·EL
12·2 KINGS
14·2 CH
7·GES
1·GENES
9·AMUEL
7·JUD

2·US
14·RONICLES
3·ITICUS
1·IS
8·RUTH
6·HUA
17·HER

FINISH

OLD TESTAMENT BOOKS OF LAW AND HISTORY

1._____   7._____   13._____

2._____   8._____   14._____

3._____   9._____   15._____

4._____   10._____   16._____

5._____   11._____   17._____

6._____   12._____

BIBLE DIVISIONS—OLD TESTAMENT LAW AND HISTORY

WALKING WITH THE ISRAELITES

Choose a number from 1 to 17. Follow the path and look for the sandals with the number you chose. Write the letters in order on the blank line with the same number. Repeat with other numbers until the blank lines are filled.

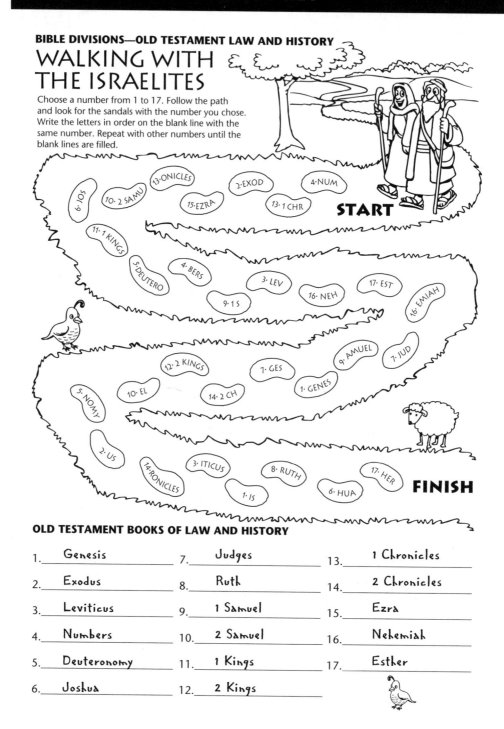

OLD TESTAMENT BOOKS OF LAW AND HISTORY

1. Genesis	7. Judges	13. 1 Chronicles
2. Exodus	8. Ruth	14. 2 Chronicles
3. Leviticus	9. 1 Samuel	15. Ezra
4. Numbers	10. 2 Samuel	16. Nehemiah
5. Deuteronomy	11. 1 Kings	17. Esther
6. Joshua	12. 2 Kings	

Maze of Scrolls

Collect all the Old Testament books of History in order. There is only one correct path.
(Hint: Use the contents page in your Bible for help.)

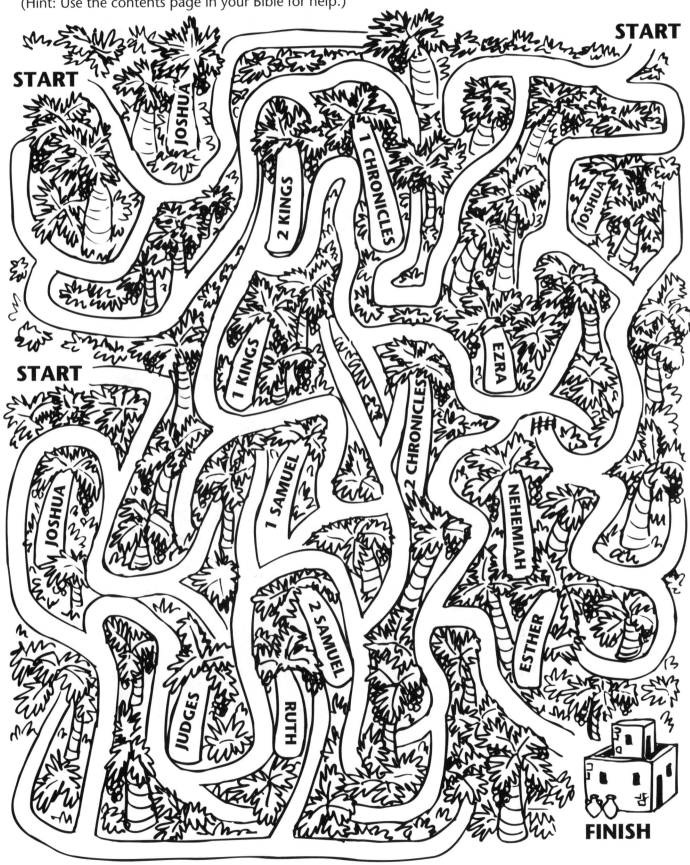

START

START

START

START

JOSHUA

2 KINGS

1 CHRONICLES

JOSHUA

EZRA

1 KINGS

2 CHRONICLES

NEHEMIAH

JOSHUA

1 SAMUEL

ESTHER

JUDGES

RUTH

2 SAMUEL

FINISH

BIBLE DIVISIONS—OLD TESTAMENT HISTORY

Maze of Scrolls

Collect all the Old Testament books of History in order. There is only one correct path.
(Hint: Use the contents page in your Bible for help.)

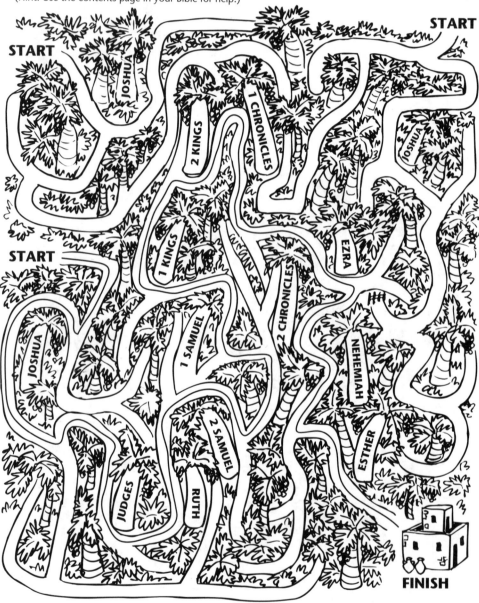

© 1999 by Gospel Light • Permission to photocopy granted. • *The Big Book of Bible Skills*

BIBLE DIVISIONS—OLD TESTAMENT HISTORY AND POETRY

KEY WORD CODE

Decode these books of History. Find the letter in the code line and then discover what it really is by looking directly below the letter in the real line. (For example, the code "SHP" is really the word "CAT.")

Tell your neighbor the other six books of History.

```
CODE:  H I S T O R Y A B C  D E F G  J K L M  N P Q U  V W X  Z
REAL:  A B C D E F G H I J  K L M N  O P Q R  S T U V  W X Y  Z
```

1. GOROFBHR: _____

2. 1 NHFQOE: ___1_____

3. CJNRQH: _____

Use the code to encode these books of History:

1. EZRR: _____

2. RUTH: _____

3. JUDGES: _____

Bonus:

Make a new code using the word "Poetry" as the key word. First write the letters of "Poetry" above the first letters of the alphabet. Then write the rest of the letters of the alphabet above the letters of the real alphabet, making sure to leave out the letters you already used in the word "Poetry." Next, try using the code you made to encode the three books of Poetry written below.

Which two books of Poetry are missing?

```
CODE:
REAL:  A B C D E F G H I J K L M N O P Q R S T U V W X Y Z
```

1. PROVERBS: _____

2. PSALMS: _____

3. ECCLESIASTES: _____

2 Samuel   1 Kings   2 Kings   1 Chronicles   2 Chronicles   Esther

BIBLE DIVISIONS—OLD TESTAMENT HISTORY AND POETRY

KEY WORD CODE

Decode these books of History. Find the letter in the code line and then discover what it really is by looking directly below the letter in the real line. (For example, the code "SHP" is really the word "CAT.")

Tell your neighbor the other six books of History.

```
CODE:  H I S T O R Y A B C  D E F G  J K L M  N P Q U  V  W X Z
REAL:  A B C D E F G H I J  K L M N  O P Q R  S T U V  W  X Y Z
```

1. GOROFBHR: __NEHEMIAH__

2. 1 NHFQOE: 1 __SAMUEL__

3. CJNRQH: __JOSHUA__

Use the code to encode these books of History:

1. EZRA: __OZMH__

2. RUTH: __MQPA__

3. JUDGES: __CQTYON__

Bonus:

Job   Song of Songs

Make a new code using the word "Poetry" as the key word. First write the letters of "Poetry" above the first letters of the alphabet. Then write the rest of the letters of the alphabet above the letters of the real alphabet, making sure to leave out the letters you already used in the word "Poetry." Next, try using the code you made to encode the three books of Poetry written below.

Which two books of Poetry are missing?

```
CODE:  P O E T R Y A B C  D F G H I  J K  L M N  Q S U V  W X  Z
REAL:  A B C D E F G H I  J K L M N  O P  Q R S  T U V W  X Y  Z
```

1. PROVERBS: __KMJURMON__

2. PSALMS: __KNPGHN__

3. ECCLESIASTES: __REEGRNCPNQRN__

Poetry Puzzler

Find the names of the books of Poetry. Write on each blank line the letter that comes between the two letters below the line.

___ ___ ___
IK NP AC

___ ___ ___ ___ ___ ___
OQ RT ZB KM LN RT

___ ___ ___ ___ ___ ___ ___ ___
OQ QS NP UW DF QS AC RT

___ ___ ___ ___ ___ ___ ___ ___ ___ ___ ___
DF BD BD KM DF RT HJ ZB RT SU DF RT

___ ___ ___ ___   ___ ___
RT NP MO FH   NP EG

BONUS: What's another name for this book?

___ ___ ___ ___ ___
RT NP MO FH RT

ANSWER KEY

BIBLE DIVISIONS—OLD TESTAMENT POETRY

Poetry Puzzler

Find the names of the books of Poetry. Write on each blank line the letter that comes between the two letters below the line.

J O B
IK NP AC

P S A L M S
OQ RT ZB KM LN RT

P R O V E R B S
OQ QS NP UW DF QS AC RT

E C C L E S I A S T E S
DF BD BD KM DF RT HJ ZB RT SU DF RT

S O N G O F
RT NP MO FH NP EG

S O N G S
RT NP MO FH RT

BONUS: What's another name for this book?

Song of Solomon

Prophet's Message

Write the answer to each question in the blank circle beside it.

How many are there?

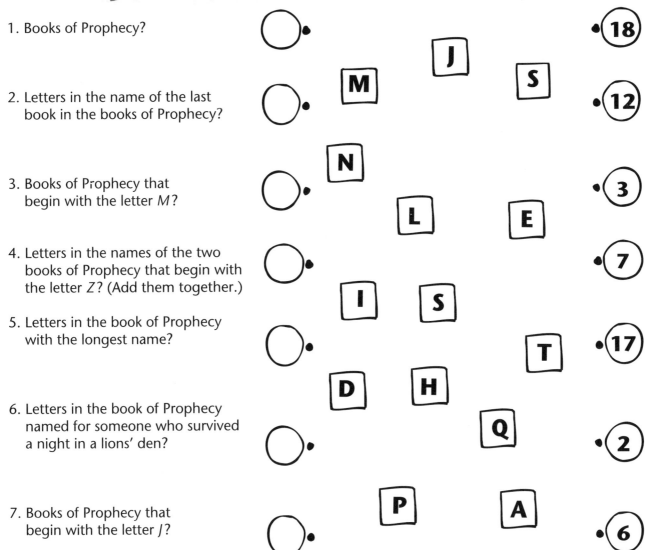

1. Books of Prophecy?

2. Letters in the name of the last book in the books of Prophecy?

3. Books of Prophecy that begin with the letter *M*?

4. Letters in the names of the two books of Prophecy that begin with the letter *Z*? (Add them together.)

5. Letters in the book of Prophecy with the longest name?

6. Letters in the book of Prophecy named for someone who survived a night in a lions' den?

7. Books of Prophecy that begin with the letter *J*?

18

12

3

7

17

2

6

Now use a ruler to draw a line between the circles with matching numbers, lining up the ruler with the dots by the circles. On the blank lines at the bottom of the page, write the letter each line passes through.

Who did the prophets say was coming?

The ___ ___ ___ ___ ___ ___ ___
      1   2   3   4   5   6   7

BIBLE DIVISIONS—OLD TESTAMENT PROPHECY

Prophet's Message

Write the answer to each question in the blank circle beside it.

How many are there?

1. Books of Prophecy?

2. Letters in the name of the last book in the books of Prophecy?

3. Books of Prophecy that begin with the letter *M*?

4. Letters in the names of the two books of Prophecy that begin with the letter *Z*? (Add them together.)

5. Letters in the book of Prophecy with the longest name?

6. Letters in the book of Prophecy named for someone who survived a night in a lions' den?

7. Books of Prophecy that begin with the letter *J*?

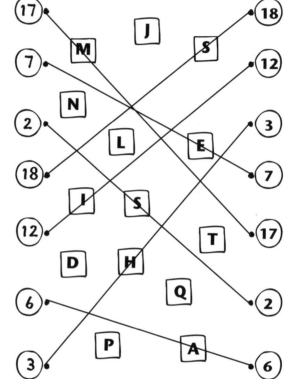

Now use a ruler to draw a line between the circles with matching numbers, lining up the ruler with the dots by the circles. On the blank lines at the bottom of the page, write the letter each line passes through.

Who did the prophets say was coming?

The M E S S I A H
1 2 3 4 5 6 7

BIBLE DIVISIONS—OLD TESTAMENT PROPHECY

Prophets' Wall

Help the prophets climb up the wall. Write the names of the books of Prophecy in the correct spaces.

Jeremiah

Ezekiel

Hosea

Isaiah

Jonah

Habakkuk

Joel

Lamentations

Zechariah

Zephaniah

Micah

Haggai

Amos

Daniel

Malachi

Nahum

Obadiah

Hint: Count the letters in each prophet's name!

BUILDER BONUS:
What groups of books come before and after the books of Prophecy?
What are the names of the five major books of Prophecy?

BIBLE DIVISIONS—OLD TESTAMENT PROPHECY

Help the prophets climb up the wall. Write the names of the books of Prophecy in the correct spaces.

Prophets' Wall

Hint: Count the letters in each prophet's name!

Jeremiah

ZEPHANIAH

Ezekiel

Isaiah

LAMENTATIONS

Hosea

Jonah

MALACHI

ISAIAH

Habakkuk

Joel

JONAH

Lamentations

Zechariah

Zephaniah

Micah

Haggai

JEREMIAH

EZEKIEL

Daniel

Amos

HABAKKUK

Malachi

Obadiah

Nahum

BUILDER BONUS:

What groups of books come before and after the books of Prophecy?
What are the names of the five major books of Prophecy?

ISAIAH, JEREMIAH, LAMENTATIONS, EZEKIEL, DANIEL

POETRY
GOSPELS

MISSING HALVES

These letters got torn in half! Find the halves of the letters that match. Write all the letters with the same pattern on a blank line. Then unscramble the letters to find the names of the divisions in the New Testament.

_____ = _____

_____ = _____

_____ = _____

_____ = _____

BIBLE DIVISIONS—NEW TESTAMENT
MISSING HALVES

These letters got torn in half! Find the halves of the letters that match. Write all the letters with the same pattern on a blank line. Then unscramble the letters to find the names of the divisions in the New Testament.

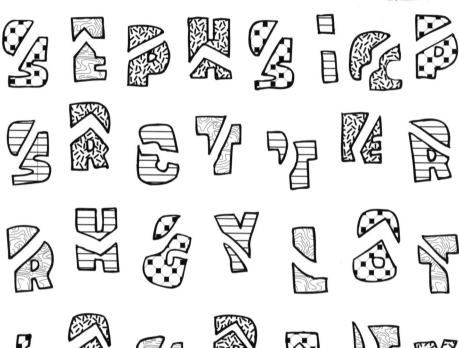

SSPGOLE	=	GOSPELS
ETRLTSE	=	LETTERS
PHCREOPY	=	PROPHECY
ISOTRHY	=	HISTORY

BALLOON POP

If you follow the directions below, you'll find out what the first division of New Testament books tell us.

Use an X to pop all balloons with

1. names of men from the Old Testament;

2. words beginning with S;

3. names of women from the New Testament;

4. names of foods eaten in Bible times.

NAME THE FOUR BOOKS IN THIS DIVISION!

Balloons:
sold, Moses, The, Gospels, figs, tell, sorry, leeks, seat, the, pomegranates, good, news, Martha, sun, of, Mary, supper, Jesus', sins, birth, bread, David, life, Aaron, teachings, onions, and, resurrection, Lydia, honey, from, Priscilla, death, on, the, Noah, cross, seven, Jacob

Write the remaining words in order on the blank lines.

_____ _____ _____ _____ _____

_____ _____ _____ _____ , _____ ,

_____ _____

_____ _____ _____ .

ANSWER KEY

BIBLE DIVISIONS—NEW TESTAMENT GOSPELS

BALLOON POP

If you follow the directions below, you'll find out what the first division of New Testament books tell us.

Use an *X* to pop all balloons with

1. names of men from the Old Testament;

2. words beginning with S;

3. names of women from the New Testament;

4. names of foods eaten in Bible times.

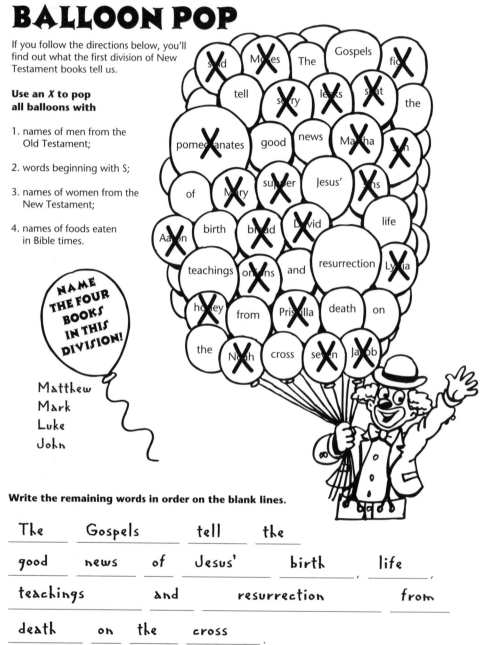

NAME THE FOUR BOOKS IN THIS DIVISION!

Matthew
Mark
Luke
John

Write the remaining words in order on the blank lines.

The   Gospels   tell   the

good   news   of   Jesus'   birth   life ,

teachings   and   resurrection   from

death   on   the   cross .

BIBLE DIVISIONS—NEW TESTAMENT LETTERS
Lost Letters

Help the letters get delivered. Collect each letter as you go through the maze.

• *The Big Book of Bible Skills*

149

BIBLE DIVISIONS—NEW TESTAMENT LETTERS

Lost Letters

Help the letters get delivered. Collect each letter as you go through the maze.

START

Ephesians
Romans
Galatians
Philippians
1, 2 Corinthians
Titus
Colossians
1, 2 Timothy
Philemon
James
1, 2 Thessalonians
1, 2, 3 John
Hebrews
Jude
1, 2 Peter

BIBLE REFERENCES

Cookie Search

Cross out all the even-numbered cookies. Then write on the blank lines the words in the odd-numbered cookies in order beginning with 1,3,5, etc. You will find out why it's important to read and study God's Word.

15 heart	**16** some	**11** in	**27** against	**12** love
9 word	**6** my	**20** Lord	**3** have	**18** wrong
21 might	**19** I	**17** that	**4** all	**13** my
25 sin	**14** soul	**2** God	**5** hidden	**10** sad
7 your	**23** not	**1** I	**8** good	**29** you

_____

_____

_____

_____. Psalm 119:11

BIBLE REFERENCES

Cookie Search

Cross out all the even-numbered cookies. Then write on the blank lines the words in the odd-numbered cookies in order beginning with 1,3,5, etc. You will find out why it's important to read and study God's Word.

I have hidden your word in my heart

that I might not sin against you.

_____

_____. Psalm 119:11

Grapevine Lines

Read the verses in your Bible. If the verse tells about God, write the reference on a grape on the left side of the vine. If the verse tells something you can do, write the reference on a grape on the right side of the vine.

God

Me

Proverbs 3:5

Psalm 86:15

Colossians 3:20   Isaiah 9:6,7   Genesis 9:15,16   Mark 16:15   James 5:13

Joshua 24:17   Jeremiah 10:12   Colossians 3:12-14   Psalm 89:1   Psalm 54:4

BIBLE REFERENCES

Grapevine Lines

Read the verses in your Bible. If the verse tells about God, write the reference on a grape on the left side of the vine. If the verse tells something you can do, write the reference on a grape on the right side of the vine.

Psalm 86:15
Isaiah 9:6,7
Genesis 9:15,16
Joshua 24:17
Jeremiah 10:12
Psalm 54:4

Proverbs 3:5
Colossians 3:20
Mark 16:15
James 5:13
Colossians 3:12–14
Psalm 89:1

God

Me

Proverbs 3:5   Psalm 86:15

Colossians 3:20   Isaiah 9:6,7   Genesis 9:15,16   Mark 16:15   James 5:13

Joshua 24:17   Jeremiah 10:12   Colossians 3:12–14   Psalm 89:1   Psalm 54:4

HIDDEN ART

Read Psalm 119:105 in your Bible. Then color yellow all the sections that contain a word from this verse. Color dark blue all the sections that contain a word that is not from this verse.

GIVE

LIFE

READ

BOOK

DOG

LOVE

GO

TRAIL

TREE

FEET

WILL

HOUSE

I

MY   IS   A

LIGHT

A

MY

WORD

LAMP

YOU

AND

PATH

MY   WORD

NEED

LIGHT

GREAT

CAT

LAW

BLUE

TEACH

WALK

GOD

CROSS

STEPS

HEART

BIBLE

Why is God's Word like the picture you discovered?

BIBLE REFERENCES

HIDDEN ART

Read Psalm 119:105 in your Bible. Then color yellow all the sections that contain a word from this verse. Color dark blue all the sections that contain a word that is not from this verse.

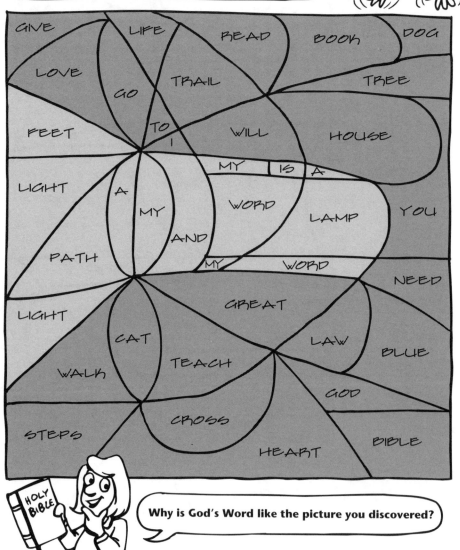

Why is God's Word like the picture you discovered?

PICTURE PARABLES

Each picture below begins with a different letter of the alphabet.
Connect the pictures in alphabetical order.

BIBLE REFERENCES

PICTURE PARABLES

Each picture below begins with a different letter of the alphabet.
Connect the pictures in alphabetical order.

A parable is a story that teaches a special lesson or truth. Jesus told lots of parables.

Read Luke 15:11-32 in your Bible to read about the picture shown above.

BIBLE REFERENCES
Star Maze

Read each reference and draw lines through the maze to connect the references which tell the same story. God sometimes used two or more people to write about the same event. That way, we have more than one chance to hear it and learn it!

Matthew 7:24-27

Mark 11:1-11

Luke 9:10-17

Matthew 21:1-11

Mark 10:46-52

Luke 6:47-49

Matthew 20:29-34

John 6:1-13

BIBLE REFERENCES

Star Maze

Read each reference and draw lines through the maze to connect the references which tell the same story. God sometimes used two or more people to write about the same event. That way, we have more than one chance to hear it and learn it!

Matthew 7:24-27

Mark 11:1-11

Matthew 21:1-11   Luke 9:10-17

Luke 6:47-49   Mark 10:46-52

Matthew 20:29-34

John 6:1-13

MAP

LANDS OF THE BIBLE

In your Bible (or a Bible atlas) find a map of Bible lands during the time when Moses led the Hebrew people out of Egypt. Use colored pencils or crayons to label your own map below.

Label and color these bodies of water:
Dead Sea (Salt Sea)
Mediterranean Sea (Great Sea)
Jordan River
Nile River
Red Sea
Sea of Galilee (Sea of Kinnereth)

Label each mountain shown by a triangle:
Mt. Ebal
Mt. Gerizim
Mt. Nebo
Mt. Sinai

Label each city shown by a dot:
Hebron
Jericho
Kadesh Barnea
Rameses

Label and color these areas or countries:
Canaan
Egypt

MAP

LANDS OF THE BIBLE

In your Bible (or a Bible atlas) find a map of Bible lands during the time when Moses led the Hebrew people out of Egypt. Use colored pencils or crayons to label your own map below.

Label and color these bodies of water:
Dead Sea (Salt Sea)
Mediterranean Sea (Great Sea)
Jordan River
Nile River
Red Sea
Sea of Galilee (Sea of Kinnereth)

Label each mountain shown by a triangle:
Mt. Ebal
Mt. Gerizim
Mt. Nebo
Mt. Sinai

Label each city shown by a dot:
Hebron
Jericho
Kadesh Barnea
Rameses

Label and color these areas or countries:
Canaan
Egypt

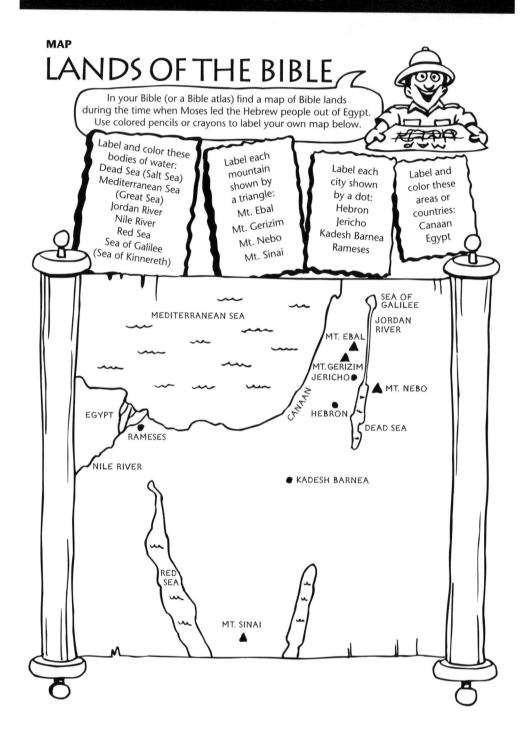

SEA OF GALILEE

MEDITERRANEAN SEA

JORDAN RIVER

MT. EBAL ▲

MT. GERIZIM
JERICHO ○

▲ MT. NEBO

CANAAN

EGYPT

HEBRON ●

DEAD SEA

RAMESES ●

NILE RIVER

● KADESH BARNEA

RED SEA

MT. SINAI ▲

MAP
Map of Miracles

1. Circle the name of the town where Jesus healed a paralyzed man. (Mark 2:1-12)

2. Draw a square around the name of the sea Jesus calmed. (Luke 8:22-26)

3. Underline the name of the town where Jesus fed 5,000 people with a boy's lunch. (Luke 9:10-17)

4. Draw an *X* by the area where Jesus healed a deaf man. (Mark 7:31-37)

5. Draw a star by the name of the town where Jesus brought a man back to life. (John 11:17-44)

6. Draw a triangle around the name of the town where Jesus changed water into wine. (John 2:1-11)

7. Draw a heart by the name of the town where Jesus healed two blind men. (Matthew 20:29-34)

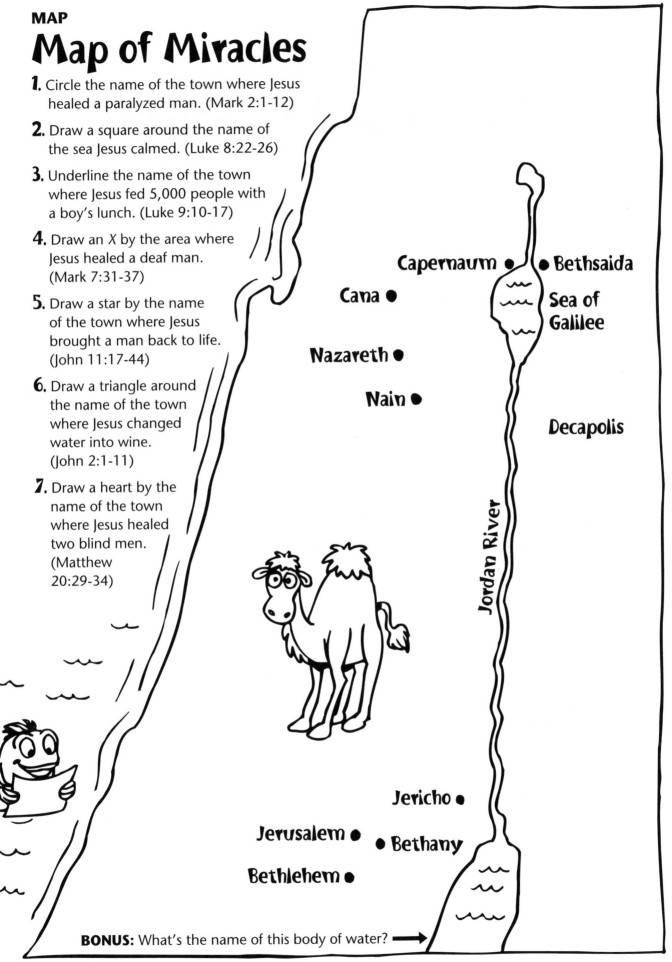

Capernaum ●   ● Bethsaida

Cana ●

Sea of Galilee

Nazareth ●

Nain ●

Decapolis

Jordan River

Jericho ●

Jerusalem ●   ● Bethany

Bethlehem ●

BONUS: What's the name of this body of water? ➞

ANSWER KEY

MAP
Map of Miracles

1. Circle the name of the town where Jesus healed a paralyzed man. (Mark 2:1-12)

2. Draw a square around the name of the sea Jesus calmed. (Luke 8:22-26)

3. Underline the name of the town where Jesus fed 5,000 people with a boy's lunch. (Luke 9:10-17)

4. Draw an X by the area where Jesus healed a deaf man. (Mark 7:31-37)

5. Draw a star by the name of the town where Jesus brought a man back to life. (John 11:17-44)

6. Draw a triangle around the name of the town where Jesus changed water into wine. (John 2:1-11)

7. Draw a heart by the name of the town where Jesus healed two blind men. (Matthew 20:29-34)

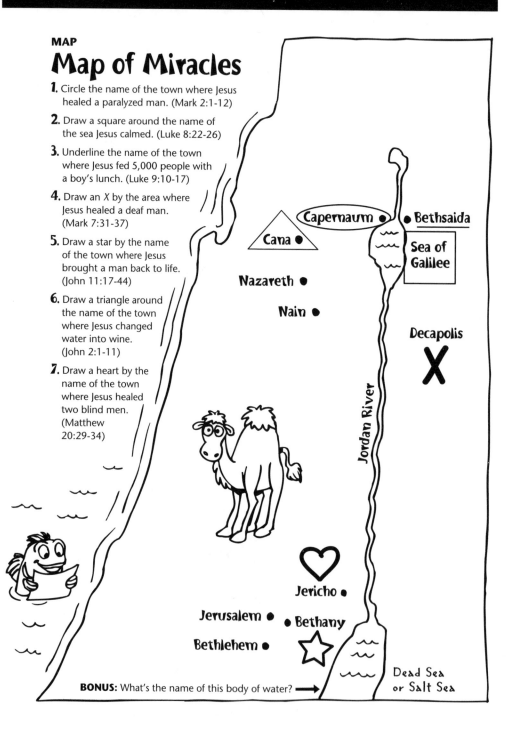

BONUS: What's the name of this body of water? ➡

MAP

Paul's Letters

The Apostle Paul wrote letters to Christians who lived in a variety of cities. Read each clue and then find the square on the map where the letter and number meet. Write the name of the city or region in that square. Draw a line from each city or region to the name of Paul's letter.

1. The region of Galatia (B9, B10).
2. The church in Rome (A1).
3. The Christians in Ephesus (C6).
4. The city of Philippi (B5).
5. Paul wrote two letters to the church in Thessalonica (B4).
6. Colossae is in D7.
7. The city of Corinth (C4).

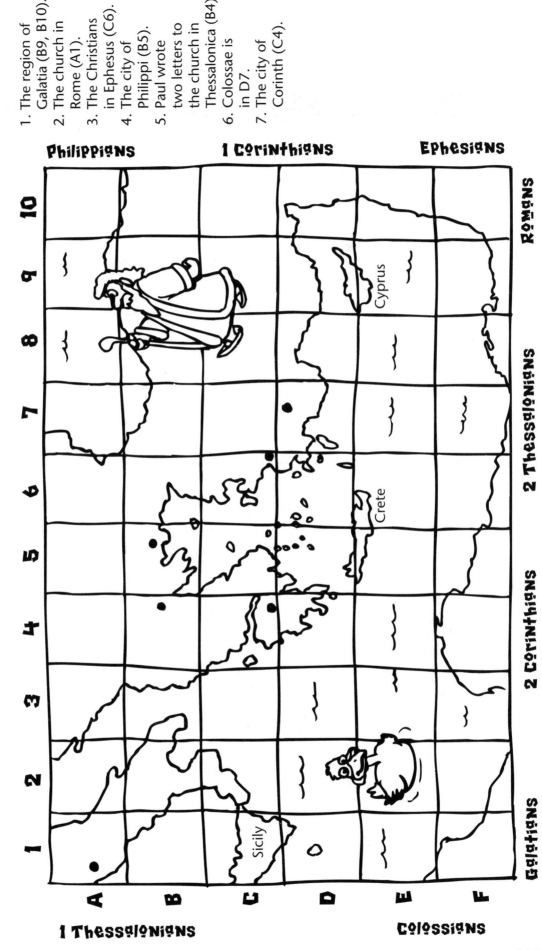

Philippians   1 Corinthians   Ephesians

Romans

2 Thessalonians

2 Corinthians

Galatians

Cyprus

Crete

Sicily

1 Thessalonians   Colossians

MAP

Paul's Letters

The Apostle Paul wrote letters to Christians who lived in a variety of cities. Read each clue and then find the square on the map where the letter and number meet. Write the name of the city or region in that square. Draw a line from each city or region to the name of Paul's letter.

1. The region of Galatia (B9, B10).
2. The church in Rome (A1).
3. The Christians in Ephesus (C6).
4. The city of Philippi (B5).
5. Paul wrote two letters to the church in Thessalonica (B4).
6. Colossae is in D7.
7. The city of Corinth (C4).

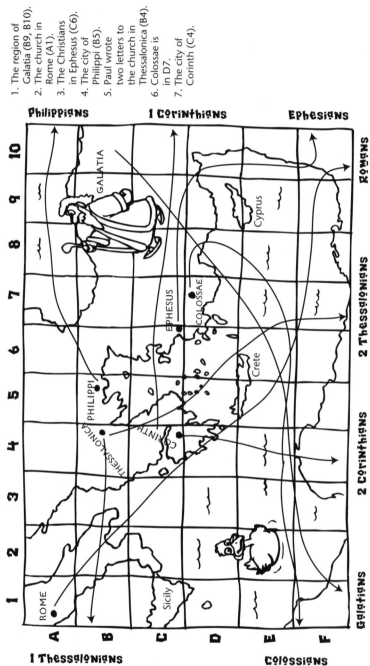

Congratulations!

You memorized _____ Bible verses!

"I have hidden your word in my heart
that I might not sin against you."
Psalm 119:11

Bible Memory Super Star

"I will hasten and not delay to obey your commands."
Psalm 119:60

Gold Ribbon Bible Memory Award

"I trust in your word." Psalm 119:42

YOU'RE AT THE TOP!

"Your word is a lamp to my feet and a light for my path."
Psalm 119:105

Bible Sleuth Award
You've discovered the treasures in God's Word!

"I love your commands more than gold, more than pure gold."
Psalm 119:127

Achievement Award
for Excellence in Bible Study

"Direct my footsteps according to your word; let no sin rule over me."
Psalm 119:133